social networking for nonprofits

Increasing Engagement in a Mobile and Web 2.0 World

ANDY STEGGLES

PUBLISHED BY ASAE & THE CENTER FOR ASSOCIATION LEADERSHIP

asae & the center™
for association leadership

WASHINGTON, DC

The authors have worked diligently to ensure that all information in this book is accurate as of the time of publication and consistent with standards of good practice in the general management community. As research and practice advance, however, standards may change. For this reason it is recommended that readers evaluate the applicability of any recommendations in light of particular situations and changing standards.

ASAE & The Center for Association Leadership
1575 I Street, NW
Washington, DC 20005-1103
Phone: (202) 626-2723; (888) 950-2723 outside the metropolitan Washington, DC area
Fax: (202) 220-6439
E-mail: books@asaecenter.org
We connect great ideas and great people to inspire leadership and achievement in the association community.

Keith C. Skillman, CAE, Vice President, Publications, ASAE & The Center for Association Leadership
Baron Williams, CAE, Director of Book Publishing, ASAE & The Center for Association Leadership

Cover design by Beth Lower, Art Director, ASAE & The Center for Association Leadership
Interior design by Troy Scott Parker, Cimarron Design

This book is available at a special discount when ordered in bulk quantities. For information, contact the ASAE Member Service Center at (202) 371-0940.

A complete catalog of titles is available on the ASAE & The Center for Association Leadership website at www.asaecenter.org.

ISBN-13: 978-0-88034-317-6
ISBN-10: 0-88034-317-6

Printed in the United States of America.

10 9 8 7 6 5 4 3 2 1

CONTENTS

ACKNOWLEDGEMENTS

I have been extremely fortunate to be supported by a loving family over the years, and this book would not have been possible without them. I would like to thank all my immediate and extended family for always being there and encouraging what are often seemingly crazy ideas and concepts and motivating me to see them through to completion.

I would specifically like to thank the following people:

- Fran, for always encouraging me to follow whatever I felt passionate about;
- Will and Campbell, my two loving children, who have sacrificed time with me so I could complete this book; and
- Mum, Dad, Simon, Sue, and James—my immediate family who have always been the greatest of cheer leaders. There are many other people who have supported me throughout the years, including the Stewart family; my friends and peers from within the association community; the staff at the Risk & Insurance Management Society, Inc. (RIMS), who I have worked closely with over the years, specifically, Val, Donna, Meg, Deb, Mary, Abe, Bronia, Christine, Sal, Vyn, Wendy, Eugene, JoAnn, and the rest of the crew; the staff at ASAE & The Center; my good friends Darren and his family; Paul Lamb, Paul Maxwell, Paul Shelly, and Anthony Roy; and last but not least, all the team at Higher Logic, by far the most progressive and inspiring company I've ever worked at.

I would also like to thank all the members of the Higher Logic User Group (the "HUG") who have been incredibly generous in reviewing random content and providing various insights and suggestions with different chapters.

Further Thanks

This book would not have been possible without help from colleagues who are not just friends but experts within the nonprofit social web arena:

- Chapter 4: Facebook, LinkedIn, and Other Outposts by Lindy Dreyer and Maddie Grant, CAE
- Chapter 5: Associations Atwitter by KiKi L'Italien
- Chapter 6: Evolving Educational Applications for Social Networking for Nonprofits by Thomas C. Stewart, PhD
- Chapter 7: Legal Risk and Liabilities on the Social Web by Barbara F. Dunn, Esq, Nathan J. Breen, and Joshua W. Peterson from Howe & Hutton, Ltd.
- Miscellaneous contributions related to the nonprofit elements of this book provided by Beaconfire Consulting

A special thank you goes to Thomas C. Stewart, PhD, who not only edited the text but also contributed a chapter.

Reviewers/Contributors

I'd like to extend thanks to the following people for either reviewing or contributing in some other way to this book.

- Kelly Flowers, Active Network
- Susan Kistler, American Evaluation Association
- Ben McClanahan, IAAP
- Angi Carr, AUVSI
- Dana Glazier, IAAM
- Peggy Hoffman, Mariner Management

INTRODUCTION

In the rapidly developing field of information technology, some forecasts uttered over the years have shown vision. Others? Not so much. In 1977, Ken Olson, founder and chairman of Digital Equipment Corporation, infamously said, "There is no reason why anyone would ever want a computer in their home."[1] While Olson may not have seen any reasons at the time, others, such as Steve Jobs and Bill Gates, certainly did. The seismic shift toward personal computers shook up the computer world in the 1980s, taking little-known companies such as Apple and Microsoft and turning them into some of the largest corporations in the world.[2,3] The explosion of social networking, social media, and mobile technologies in recent years represents another change in computing with the potential to be as profound as the personal computer revolution.

Social networks have been around for years, but the convergence of Web 2.0, social networks, social media, and more recently, mobile technologies, along with the quest for organic/natural search engine traffic has led to the explosion of a new generation of applications that are fast, intuitive, and for the most part, self-generating. This disruptive innovation is known as social networking, informal communities that are part of the vast social web spawned by the internet.

Introducing the Social Networking and Media Association (SNAMA)

In 2006, just two years after Facebook was founded, I discussed with colleagues in the nonprofit community the question of whether a group created in Facebook constituted an association. At first, the thought was more of a joke than anything else, but as Facebook exploded in popularity and thousands of groups were created, the question became more relevant. As a result, I decided to conduct a little experiment. I created a group within Facebook and called it an association—the Social Networking and Media Association (SNAMA). After the group had grown to more than 300 people, I went back to my trusted group of colleagues and asked them again if it was an association (because I had called it one). After long debates discussing things like the group's lack of structure, bylaws, dues, and overall governance, I decided to create a website for the group. In 2008, www.SNAMA.org was born—a free association for anyone interested in the social web.

There are many definitions of what a "Facebook group" is considered to be, but essentially, it is an informal group of people with a common interest. This is very similar to the IRS definition of what an association is: "...a group of persons banded together for a specific purpose."[4] Clearly there is overlap of what the two are. It is important to note that associations do not need to register as nonprofits, but most do because it often provides a tax advantage.

With so many potential associations being formed in public social networks, it is only a matter of time before a new type of association is created: Association 2.0. SNAMA has been modeled around the principles of the social web (open, collaborative, lack of structure, and other traits) with the goals of a more traditional association (to have a formal presence). The goal of this model is to remain both nimble and sustainable while fulfilling the organization's mission and objectives.

SNAMA charges no dues. Before being formalized by the Executive Committee, the mission was originally created using a wiki, which has evolved through member input into what it is today. There is no board of directors or bylaws. There is simply a small executive committee that is empowered to do what it sees fit, understanding that it must be in the best interests of the organization and enforce the mission (which can easily be changed). Within a year, SNAMA had grown by word of mouth to more than 1,000 members and continues to grow. The organization is managed by a typical association management software system that is paid for by sponsorship ads within the eGroup discussions and elsewhere in the site.

SNAMA is a great example of how the power of the social web can be leveraged by others to potentially compete with a nonprofit's offerings and diminish the traditional value of its membership. New, less formal associations that are beginning to appear have little overhead, structure, or formality and often no dues. Most importantly, they are nimble enough to grasp opportunity.

Using Social Media to Your Advantage

My hope would be that this book helps nonprofit leaders compete in this forthcoming world of Association 2.0. This book intends to focus on two core audiences—social consumers and social producers—and one emerging technology, mobile. It has been designed to cater to those who are new to social networking and social media as well as those who fully understand the basic principles and how to use them but are wondering what to do next. The book is specifically targeted to nonprofits, with particular emphasis on professional and trade associations, societies, and other member- or donor-based communities. While most of the examples given are related to associations, application to a society, charity, or charitable foundation is usually appropriate. Similarly, the term "members," in most cases, can also be substituted with "donors" or "volunteers." Although not the intended purpose, most of the principles of this book can also be applied to the for-profit world.

Social Consumers

Social consumers are the people who want to learn how to participate in or set up a social group or network. These are people who may have never heard of Facebook or LinkedIn but are interested in knowing what all the hype is about and where they should start.

The first part covers these areas: What is the social web? Where do you find it? What are the core components? How do you use it? How do you listen to it? How do you attract new members, retain existing members, and build on community? The rest of the first section then discusses in detail the legal issues and liability concerns most nonprofits have regarding social media, the threats and opportunities of public versus private networks, and how mobile is changing everything.

Social Providers

Social providers typically are organizations that want to leverage their existing network of members, donors, subscribers, and other constituents to collaborate more effectively. In most cases, this means using a private social network.

This section assumes the reader is already familiar with the social consumer concepts explained in the first part of the book and with the principles of a private (white-label) social network. The correlation and the importance of the search engines with social media will be explained as well as how to generate significant nondues revenue using innovative social web-based ideas. A large part of this section is dedicated to how to measure, recognize, and reward engagement, providing specific examples. Readers will be shown how to leverage components as part of their plan by generating engagement and nondues revenue and improving member satisfaction. The final part of the book takes you through a typical platform selection process for a private network. It concludes with a detailed look at how to launch the platform, providing a sample marketing launch plan and a detailed explanation of the Go-to-Market strategies.

There are numerous examples of social providers and how this can work:

- The American Bar Association might want to create a social network for attorneys who focus on different aspects of law.
- The publishers of "Biotech Weekly" might want to provide greater subscriber benefits for their subscribers by providing a platform for readers to network with each other or discuss recently published articles or the industry in general.
- ASAE & The Center might want to create social networks that allow readers of its various publications to network with each other.
- An event management company might want to provide a social platform for attendees of an annual show it produces.

Mobile Technologies

By 2013, mobile phones will overtake PCs as the most common web access device worldwide.[5] This being the case, mobile should have a significant consideration as part of your overall social strategy. With this in mind, one chapter of this book has been dedicated to giving a detailed overview of mobile, its implications for associations, and the various options which associations have to take.

References

1. Maney, K. Tech titans wish we wouldn't quote them on this baloney. USAToday.com, July 5, 2005.
2. Getting personal. *The Economist*, July 29, 2006. 57-58.
3. Thurber, Jr., K. T. Buried bytes: A history of the personal computer. *Popular Electronics 12 (4)*, April, 1995. 36-43.
4. http://www.irs.gov/charities/article/0,,id=96120,00.html.
5. By 2013, mobile phones will overtake PCs as the most common Web access device worldwide. www.gartner.com, Gartner, January 13, 2010.

CHAPTER 1

The Basics of Social Networking

Social networking has been around in one form or another for years. Many nonprofits have chapters or donors who regularly meet to learn, network, or generally do good. This is the most primitive form of social networking (in-person). Other types of networking have evolved with the technologies that enable them. For years, the future of networking was assumed to be synchronous (real time) networking in different locations. It turns out that this is not the case.

The Social Web Explosion

Social networking really started to take off when technology became so easy to use that people didn't realize they were doing anything out of the ordinary. Typically, a person would receive an invitation from a friend or colleague who set up a LinkedIn profile and invited all of his or her friends to join as well. At about the same time, MySpace and Friendster started to take off and people started to connect with other people via these sites as well. People didn't realize they were "social networking" at the time, since their mission was to accept a "Friend" request or a "Community Invitation" from a peer. The fact that all of these actions constituted social networking was far from relevant.

Once the hype settled and Facebook had made its appearance (originally exclusively for college students), the world started to pay attention to what social networking was all about. As a result of uploading their address books or adding email addresses into Facebook, users started accepting "Friend" requests. By virtue of accepting a friend request, you have joined the social network. Shortly thereafter, those same people would start to receive suggestions about others they should friend and network with as well as others they might not know but who have interests in common.

Just a couple of years after Facebook really took off it reached more than 200 million users from around the globe. (It's now at more than 350 million and continues to grow.[1]) Facebook calls itself a "social utility" mostly because it doesn't want to pigeonhole itself into being recognized as a social networking platform—it's really a social *everything* platform.

In 1999, I designed a system that allowed members to search and send other members a message while storing the message in their online inbox. Members could search the directory, add other members to their "list" and ultimately send them all an email. This type of functionality was pretty typical then. However, with the onset of Web 2.0 technologies, the user experience became much less complicated and the dreams and ideas of the late 90s suddenly started to catch attention. When the user experience was so simple that anyone could do it, people not only noticed but became engaged. People would join the social networks, find people, and initiate collaborative engagements (friend request, event invitation, or other experiences).

What Is Social Media?

While social networking is all about "friending" (connecting with others and building relationships), social media is all about sharing content through blogs (blogger.com), videos (youtube.com), podcasts (apple.com/itunes), or just commenting on an article in the *New York Times*.

In its simplest form, social media is about user-generated content (UGC). Think of UGC as information created or shared by a member, donor, or other constituent. UGC is not just creating blog postings or wiki edits or uploading YouTube videos; it's all of the above and more. The most prevalent part of social media is the sharing of content. Content is not just about sharing thoughts and ideas, however; it's also about sharing an experience. For example, imagine you've just read a blog and then are compelled enough (in a positive or negative way) to rate this particular blog. You are still taking part in the social media experience. You are generating content whether you like it or not. After all, the next person who comes along will view the newly aggregated rating. Since your rating was received, the aggregated rating might have moved up from 4.1 out of 5 to 4.2 out of 5. By taking this action you have contributed to the social media UGC experience.

Take this a step further and consider what a contribution is. Writing or rating a blog is contributory in nature, as is reviewing or commenting on a blog and rating a comment on a blog. But what about people who simply view/read a blog? Lurking or spectating, as it's known, is the most popular activity of all, and if people weren't viewing content, creators would likely not create it. Even spectators add to the UGC by simply being a demographic. When you watched the "Evolution of Dance" video on YouTube.com, you may see that you are the 143rd millionth person to watch it. This demographic is displayed to all users. The demographic itself is not very useful, but it does demonstrate a level of engagement around this particular piece of content and, therefore, might compel someone to watch a video or read a blog simply because so many other people have watched or read it. To some degree, all of these actions constitute UGC and together make up the social media experience.

The ability to rate and review content underscores a whole new philosophy. A traditional marketing or communications professional is used to having a reasonable degree of control over a brand. After all, they decide what to publish, and they are the only ones who see any complaints or other types of feedback provided to the organization, usually through letters or emails. With the onset of social media, these same professionals suddenly have little or no control over who sees what feedback. Suddenly, every person and organization is accountable to the rest of the world. Marketing and communications professionals have to give up some control and adapt to the new era of the social web.

What Is Web 2.0?

Web 2.0 is not really any single technology or process. It is a term given to a whole new generation of technologies. The idea is that the web has come so far, so fast that the experience of an end user is very different today than it was just a couple of years ago. Yet there are many websites and programs that have not changed since the days of the late '90s dotcom boom. To differentiate the old from the new (in terms of usability and functionality) the term Web 2.0, coined by Tim O'Reilly (http://www.oreillynet.com/pub/au/27), essentially means a whole new generation of technologies which really advance the user experience.

Example of Web 2.0—AJAX

A simple but important example of this type of technology is AJAX, which stands for Asynchronous Javascript And XML. AJAX allows servers and computers to talk behind the scenes. While this may not seem important for the end user (the web surfer), it can have a huge impact on their experience.

For example, in the Web 1.0 world, if you went to a website that asked you to rate an article, you would perhaps click on the fourth star out of five. Then the entire page would have reloaded and you would have been presented with a new page that said, "Thank you for rating. Click here to return or go back," or something equally time consuming. It's interesting that we think this is time consuming. A decade ago most users would have expected such a process and not thought much of it. This is one reason why most people would never have clicked on the rating itself. (Why waste the time?). With AJAX, a user can click on a rating and instead of the entire page refreshing and reloading (sending the rating to the server and asking the server to send the entire page again), the webpage simply sends a single message to the server saying, "Hey, Andy has rated this as 4 out of 5. What do I do next?" The answer would be something like, "Tell him 'thanks' and show him the new aggregated rating, which is 4.2."

As an end user, you simply clicked on the fourth star and the page didn't move (no reloading). Instead you'd get a "Thanks for Rating" message and a few seconds later, this same message changed to the new aggregated rating of "4.2 out of 5 (based on 231 ratings)." The important thing is that the page didn't reload and the user experience was not interrupted. From a programmer's perspective, the server did not have to resend an identical page just to display a couple of words different from what the user saw previously. This not only improves the user experience but also has a huge positive impact on website performance as well as bandwidth utilization.

Summary: The Social Web

The social web underscores a paradigm shift in conventional thinking with regard to authenticity and trust and a general shift in power to the consumer. In the Web 1.0 days, typical non-tech-savvy consumers who had problems with a product would have written a complaint to the supplier. If they were really unsatisfied, they might have gone a step further and reported them to a Better Business Bureau or some other trusted or regulatory body. Today, all that has changed. Consumers know they can now go to the web, search for the offending product, and find the top result, which will almost always offer visitors the chance to comment/rate/review. The power has suddenly been put in the consumer's hands. If a supplier offends the consumer, the consumer can let the entire world know. If the offending action is particularly egregious, then the consumer's report may very well go viral such as the United Breaks Guitars video on YouTube.com.

While there are other elements to the social web, such as social bookmarking, crowd sourcing, and mashups, to some degree they all fall under one of the broader categories of social networking or social media. Social networking and social media in a Web 2.0 world constitute what we now know as the social web.

Case Study: Phi Sigma Sigma

Phi Sigma Sigma is a 60,000-member, international sorority with more than 100 alumnae groups and collegiate chapters active at colleges and universities across the United States and Canada. As a social and philanthropic entity, Phi Sigma Sigma's mission is to instill the values of leadership through service, lifelong learning, and social inclusiveness in today's young women and future leaders. Members join Phi Sigma Sigma during their college years and stay active in the organization long after graduating. Phi Sigma Sigma offers many benefits to its members, including leadership programs, active clubs, and special events for alumnae. The staff of Phi Sigma Sigma is small, with 10 people handling financial issues, membership services, and information technology initiatives. Therefore, many of Phi Sigma Sigma's collegiate and alumnae programs and activities are lead by volunteers. The leadership of Phi Sigma Sigma saw an opportunity through the new world of collaborative social media to bring together its staff, members, and volunteers to share resources, stay connected, and offer new ways to engage collegiate members and alumnae. The resulting social network has been successful beyond expectations, and Phi Sigma Sigma has forever changed the way it conducts member business.

Challenge

Phi Sigma Sigma began to notice the emergence and rapid adoption of social media tools, especially within their collegiate demographic, so it was essential to make social networking an integral part of the sorority experience. More than 5,500 of Phi Sigma Sigma's collegiate members were already using Facebook, so it was a natural progression to implement a social networking program as an organizational offering. While Phi Sigma Sigma had some simple social networking tools already in place, it wanted to expand its solution to support a comprehensive member directory and recognition program, blogging, resource library, community calendars, and chapter websites. In addition to implementing a social networking solution, Phi Sigma Sigma also needed to redesign and relaunch its website. The social media community site and tools needed to be seamlessly integrated with Phi Sigma Sigma's back-end membership system as well as the new website.

Evaluation
The leadership of Phi Sigma Sigma had clear objectives when evaluating available social networking tools. Of paramount importance was to select a solution that was fully integrated to their association management system (AMS). Phi Sigma Sigma opted for a private community platform they called Connected Community, which recognized the importance of a single source for data management, thereby eliminating the need for members to update information in more than one place.

Quick Facts

Organization Type: Fraternal Organization

Membership Types: Individual

Number of Members: 60,000

Location: Elkridge, Maryland, USA

Mission: To inspire the personal development of each sister and perpetuate the advancement of womanhood.

Vision: To be a dynamic sisterhoood of powerful women fostering uncompromising principles, igniting change, and embracing individuality.

Success Story
Within the scope of the website redesign and social media solution, the guiding business objectives of Phi Sigma Sigma included redefining and streamlining the way the organization did business and expanding its online offerings to their collegiate and alumnae members. During the implementation of the selected platform, Phi Sigma Sigma discovered that through design and use, social networking was emerging as the core of its new website, with site content and functionality weaved into the collaboration tools. For its newly designed corporate website, Phi Sigma Sigma used microsites to build out the menu structure and content. Microsites afforded Phi Sigma Sigma a flexible, easy-to-use content management tool to effectively manage its web presence. In addition to its organizational site, Phi Sigma Sigma rolled out microsites to each of its chapters, allowing Phi Sigma Sigma to effectively manage the brand by controlling the visual identity of each chapter.

Because Phi Sigma Sigma is a highly social philanthropic organization and its membership is exclusively female, the leadership wanted to present collegians and alumnae with a way to connect with other members and form ad-hoc communities of interest. The directory module allowed Phi Sigma Sigma's members to see a full profile of each member, including interests, work experience, contact information, and communities of practice. Phi Sigma Sigma's membership can now find other like-minded members, reconnect with old friends, and network in new ways.

Revenue for Phi Sigma Sigma was historically based on collections from collegiate members. However, two years ago, Phi Sigma Sigma launched a voluntary alumnae dues program, encouraging alumnae to donate to help cover the costs of their new initiatives. To recognize these donors, Phi Sigma Sigma now awards them a Loyal Sister Badge on their member profile. The positive recognition of individual sisters has helped to foster an environment of giving.

Results

The cost savings from implementing Phi Sigma Sigma's Connected Community was realized almost immediately. Their resource library module has allowed executive and chapter leaders to share and collaborate on documents that historically needed to be printed, bound, and shipped. Additionally, executive and chapter leaders needed to travel to meet for reviewing documents. Now, all documents are reviewed and commented on online, eliminating the need for travel or printing costs. The rollout and successful adoption of the Connected Community suite and social networking strategy have had a significant and meaningful impact within Phi Sigma Sigma's membership. Through the use of a comprehensive community site, Phi Sigma Sigma has reengineered the way it does business and virtually eliminated the need for paper work and clerical staff. With the introduction of two new monthly e-newsletters, Phi Sigma Sigma provides valuable content that is linked back to their website, making the organizational online portal more and more the single source of information for all things Phi Sigma Sigma.

Fortunately, Phi Sigma Sigma had executive sponsorship that cleared the path for the successful implementation. The social strategy and rollout plan included requiring all new members to agree to organizational policies, pay dues, and conduct member business exclusively through the website. As a result, almost the entire collegiate base and thousands of alumnae are now a part of the social network. Already socially enabled, Phi Sigma Sigma has managed to make their online world sociable.

As Lisa Moshkovich, Phi Sigma Sigma's membership manager, says, "The technology on our website that is available to our Phi Sigma Sigma sisters is amazing. The resource libraries and discussion forums have made the management of our collegiate and alumnae chapters much easier—less time for the staff to process reports and more information available to our members and volunteers in real time. We are always aware of what is going on."

Reference

1. http://www.facebook.com/press/releases.php#!/press/releases.php?p=133917.

CHAPTER 2

Characteristics of a Social Platform

Facebook, LinkedIn, and private social networks have similar core characteristics. There are numerous features within the different social networks, so this chapter focuses on features which are most relevant to nonprofits and discusses how features differ between public and private social networks.

Personal Profile

Everyone who joins a social network automatically has a personal profile. LinkedIn is really trying to push personal profiles as professional profiles. Similar to LinkedIn, associations and nonprofits are trying to emphasize the professional nature of a social network. This does make sense when you think about it; after all, if someone has a profile on LinkedIn and is a professional working in the utilities industry, then why not have the professional profile on the association website that best represents the respective industry (your association)?

Social networks have similar common characteristics when it comes to the professional profile: name, [partial] address/location, job title, company, email, school, and other elements.

With Facebook, the main part of the profile would be these fields plus things like your marital status and other personal information. However, with LinkedIn and private social networks, the emphasis is on areas such as the person's bio, professional memberships , certifications, and similar professional information.

In a private social network, a professional profile is much more dynamic, showing more active information about what an individual has been doing (e.g., Andy attended the 2006 New York chapter workshop on social technologies, served on the technology task force in 2007, and was part of the membership committee from 2007 to 2009). Combine this with certifications, purchase history, and other demographics, and suddenly you have a much more holistic professional profile for people to view. Think of it as a constantly evolving, live professional resume. In this instance, the resume on the association website is based on behavioral data versus the resume on LinkedIn, which is based on what the user has provided.

In a public network, the engagement data is limited because it only knows what you tell it, such as, I have this degree, I attended this course, I know these people, and I have these interests.

Here are a few examples of professional profiles on a private versus public social network:

NYSAE: http://www.nysaenet.org/andysteggles
SNAMA: http://www.SNAMA.org/AndySteggles
LinkedIn: http://www.linkedin.com/in/steggles

In a private social network, the profile data itself is less important than the networking opportunities it represents. Consider this when you look at your profile: With one click, you can connect with an entire class from a course you took back in 2004 or a task force you worked on in 2006. In a less membership-specific example, consider how Amazon now lets you connect with people who purchased similar products and services. All of this revolves around an active profile that is built on engagement. This type of profile can be much more valuable than the typical profile you might see in a more traditional online or printed member directory.

Friending

Friending is all about establishing a trust relationship with another person. Typically when you take part in a social network you do so because you were invited by a friend or peer. When you accept the invitation and establish your profile, you are then immersed in an online connected community. Among other things, you are then able to connect with friends of your friends. While this might not sound like a big deal, it essentially extends your personal network exponentially.

One thing to note about friending: The public social networks usually refer to "Add Friend" as opposed to the private social networks, which tend to use words that are perceived as more professional, such as colleague, peer, or contact. This is only semantic, but it is something to be aware of. What would your members, alumni, or donors respond to better?

To initiate a friend request, you normally search for people based on name, location, demographic, or activity. When you find the people you want to connect with, you send a friend request, and if you don't know them, you might add a little introduction about why you are trying to connect with them. You can't see the recipient's full profile until they have accepted your request, at which time a new trust level is established and you can see a more complete profile.

While this may sound pretty straightforward, there are gray areas. What if you have all your college photos on your Facebook account and your boss tries to "friend" you? Do you remove the hundreds of photos, wall postings, and other seemingly harmless, but professionally negative, content from your profile? Facebook joined a few other social networks to address this very issue. After it realized that many people were creating duplicate profiles for business and personal use, Facebook built in the ability to add people to specific lists (categories) and then assign different permissions to each category. This allows a user to have a professional category for work colleagues and a personal category for family and friends. You can restrict the professional category so its members can't see your personal information, only the things you want them to see.

How Do They Know Who My Friends Are?

I'm often asked by people, "How does Facebook so accurately figure out who I might know or want to know?" For example, if you just created your first account on Facebook, you'd enter basic information such as your name, email address, and password. But then Facebook may present you with possible matches of people you may want to connect with and the majority of time, they are valid. Since you supplied only the most basic information, how could they possibly come up with the possible matches?

There are many explanations for this, but the one which tends to resonate well is when people start getting into Facebook, they often upload their address book to help look for matches. Facebook records that you had this specific set of email addresses. While it may not have found a match for some of them, when any of those people eventually do create their profile for the first time, Facebook remembers that you had their email address in your address book; it then recognizes that you are probably a good match for them in terms of being a possible friend/contact.

This suggestion/matching technique is employed by both public and private social networks and is a great way to generate viral engagement and participation.

Communities and Networks

When you join a social network, you'll normally be taken through some sort of wizard that asks you a set of questions to help get you started, for instance; When did you graduate from college? and What discipline was your degree focus? etc. This is a good example of what distinguishes networks and communities.

Facebook has networks of like people that are formed around colleges and universities and segmented by year and discipline. These networks are dynamically created, and most people are attached to them as part of the sign-up process. A network is different from a community. A community can be a group or a fan page, which are similar. (A fan page is open to the search engines; a group is not.) While a network is dynamically driven, a community is normally created by a user who sends invitations to friends to join the community.

In the nonprofit world, networks are much more prevalent in private communities and tend to work well around industry-specific demographic information. For example, if I were on a private community site for risk managers, I might be asked in which countries I have offshore operations. If I were to select Brazil, then the moment I click on save, the system would look to see if there is anyone else like me who has dealings in Brazil. If so, it will build a network of like people.

Imagine how many opportunities there are for networking. Gone are the days when a nonprofit would ask constituents for their demographics for the sole purpose of sending them spam (or targeted marketing as we like to call it); instead, the value proposition has changed. Now a member or donor is asked to provide demographics in order to help them network. Each time participants give you a little information, the system adds them to respective networks, enabling them to connect with others and to be connected to others more efficiently.

Communities, on the other hand, can be more powerful then networks. Because a community is deliberately created by an engaged member, it already has a champion. The champion is responsible for nurturing the community and making it grow. A community may have many properties. The most basic community may be a list of people but may not actually do anything. A more engaged community might have discussion groups (eGroups), libraries, events, and possibly its own website.

When creating a community, consider what types of communities your association may need. For example, a private social network used by an association might have the following communities:

- Committees (board of directors, technology committee, membership committee)
- Chapters (New York chapter, Florida chapter)
- Regions (Northwest, Midwest)
- Special Interest Groups (SIGs) (manufacturing, retail)
- Events (people who have registered or attended specific events)
- Member-Created Group (non-sanctioned/official member-created groups)

Different rules may be associated with each community type. For example, committees might have restricted access and be invitation only (nobody can join unless invited—exclusivity). Chapters might all have their own community websites. Regions are dynamic; if you live in New York, you are immediately added to the Northeast region. Other types of attributes associated with communities are things like the default email subscription frequency or format (real time versus daily digest in an HTML versus Plain Text or mobile friendly format). The attributes given to a community are dictated by its mission.

Networks can be as simple as pre-canned search criteria with the ability to connect other participants, while communities typically take engagement to a higher level.

Blogs

Blogs are "Basic Logs" and are typically a more informal way of publishing opinions or news. The blogs around the web are collectively known as the "Blogosphere" and consist of more than 100 million blogs [http://en.wikipedia.org/wiki/Technorati]. From an association perspective, blogs are often confused with listservers or forums. While there is definitely some overlap, blogs are usually unsolicited opinions in the form of informal articles, while the more traditional listserver or forum is often used to ask a question or provide an answer.

If you are considering starting a blog, it's important to understand blogging etiquette. There are some informal rules about producing a successful blog. Consider this analogy: When you are at a party, pretend you are holding a ball, and you are not allowed to hold the ball longer than anyone else. The ball represents who is talking, and it is a simple way of making sure you are not overwhelming the rest of the group. The blogosphere has similar characteristics in a sense that most topics/industries are composed of close-knit communities that often give opinions that are referenced on their respective blogs.

When you arrive at a dinner party, and you don't know anyone yet, it is not likely you would just start talking over others. Normally you would introduce yourself, get to know the other guests and then casually start up a conversation with them. The blogosphere works in a similar way. If you are a newbie and have never commented on a blog for a specific topic before, it is unlikely anyone will pay much attention to you if you simply jump in and ask people to link to your blog.

If you start a blog, the first thing to understand is who else is blogging. You can find out by doing simple searches using a blog search engine such as www.google.com/blogsearch or http://technorati.com.

Once you find the bloggers, you need to start following them by subscribing to their blogs. As they post new content that is interesting to you, comment with your opinion. This will act as a subtle introduction for you. Once you've spent a while commenting on the industry bloggers, you should then start blogging yourself. Don't worry about who will see it, since the search engines will pick it up and the bloggers will most likely have alerts set up to let them know if any new industry news is found. As Google finds your blog, it will alert other bloggers who will look at it in their own time. When they see your name and recognize you as the person who has been commenting on their blogs, the odds are they will comment on and link to your blog.

This is just the beginning, but an important, step to being recognized within the community. As a known blogger reads your blog and then blogs about it, everyone who reads that blog will see a link to your blog. This is the start of becoming part of your blogger community.

When blogging remember these key points:

1. Don't blog for the sake of it. Post content if it could be truly valuable to the community.
2. Research your topic. The last thing you want to do is post a blog about a given topic only to find out your facts are wrong. Other bloggers will react negatively if you do this.
3. Set expectations and declare how often you intend to blog—every day, week, month.
4. Be patient. Don't be overly intrusive trying to get into the community
5. When linking, don't show the web address; instead, ensure you link text. For example:

   Don't show:

   > If you are looking for social networking information, go to www.snama.org.

Instead, show:

> The Social Networking and Media Association is a great source of information on the social web.

In the above example, the words are linked. This tells the search engines the site that is being referenced is related to the words "Social Networking and Media Association" and linked. This is extremely valuable to bloggers. (See Chapter 9 about search engines and the social web for more details on this.)

Remember that blogs are typically brief and to the point. Don't repeat a lot of content; instead, just link to the original source and summarize when necessary. The blogosphere is all about links, since this is what plays well with the search engine rankings. The more links to your blog, the higher you will appear in the search results. "Link love" is a good thing, and you should do what you can to get links to your site in a meaningful, legitimate way.

Forums, Listservers, and eGroups

While blogs are for posting unsolicited opinions, forums, listservers, and eGroups are for asking questions. In a Web 1.0 world, people subscribed to email lists where people posted messages and the system would then send that message to all the subscribers. (Usually people opt for the digest version which is where the system collates all the messages on a given day into a single email and then sends it out.)

Forums came after listservers and were supposed to be the next generation of discussion groups. Forums tended to work well for more technically inclined users but often failed for more tech-challenged users. The primary reason for failure was that most forums didn't have email capability. The assumption was for the user to go to the website to look for new messages. Activity typically dropped significantly because people just forgot, didn't have time, or simply couldn't be bothered to go to the web to ask their question, post their response, or review the latest postings.

A few years later a Web 2.0 technology merged both the traditional listserver and slightly more modern forum media into a new technology called "eGroups." Now the forum functionality is available on the web but that same format and functionality is also emailed to the subscribers, creating a real Web 2.0 experience. eGroups can be a revenue generator, since email and its respective website typically allow for banner advertising that, for very targeted lists, can be an attractive proposition if priced correctly.

When considering how to launch an eGroups system, consider these most important components:

1. The frequency and format you want members to receive the messages
2. Whether you should auto-subscribe the members
3. How many eGroups you will have

Frequency depends on the group. For example, if you are setting up an eGroup for your board of directors, they typically like to receive content in real time. On the other hand, a special interest group with thousands of people would probably be better served by a daily digest. In all cases, the HTML version provides a much better usability experience for the member, so unless they are on a mobile device that does not render HTML well (such as older Blackberries), then you would set the default description to be HTML format.

When considering auto-subscription, the answer is almost always yes. In my experience, communities that start with only invites have taken significantly longer to get going—if they took off at all. The keys to subscribing members are: 1) don't subscribe them to many different lists; 2) don't subscribe them to the real-time version if they are part of a large group; and 3) subscribe only people you have an established relationship with (your members, donors, or alumni, for example). Limits to autosubscribing are particularly important because your constituents don't want to be overwhelmed with emails.

The final key consideration is how many eGroups should be created. Often associations create one generic, catch-all eGroup and then perhaps one eGroup for each special interest group. While there is no right answer, generally speaking it is a best practice to either have a generic eGroup or special interest eGroups, but not both. If you have both, what usually happens is that everyone gravitates to the larger, generic eGroup and they often forget about the smaller, more targeted eGroups.

Wikis

Wikis were popularized by Wikipedia.org, a free, nonprofit multilingual web-based encyclopedia that contains content built on an open-edit model. Since its launch in 2001, the site has grown to more than 10 million articles in 250 languages, which have been written by, and for, the public.[1]

A wiki is a collaborative environment where people can edit and update web pages with relative ease. To edit a page, you simply go to the page and click on edit, make the change(s) and then click on save. Some wiki-based websites don't even require you to login.

While making changes is relatively easy, it is often difficult if you wish to add any sort of formatting such as bulleted text or adding hyperlinks to areas within the same or other pages. Wikipedia is built using "MediaWiki," a powerful wiki-building software tool.

While wikis have remained relatively similar in terms of the concept of allowing anyone to edit, there are many variations of how this can work. For example, many wiki software applications no longer require you to know how to use the wiki syntax to format text; instead, they are using the easier WYSIWYG (What You See Is What You Get) editor. Also, while the original Wikipedia model had a single purpose—to build an encyclopedia, wikis are being used for many other purposes, some equally as broad but many much narrower in scope, such as an industry specific glossary of terms/phrases/acronyms etc.

Nonprofit Uses for Wikis

Nonprofit user groups might use a wiki for product documentation that is maintained "by the community, for the community." Associations are using wikis to replace their more traditional paper-based glossaries of terms/phrases/acronyms for their respective industries or interests. Some associations are updating their list of FAQs to use a wiki format, so their members can help update them. When I created www.SNAMA.org, I used a wiki environment to capture member thoughts on where the direction of the organization should go. To do this, I turned the mission of the organization into a wiki and invited people to update it however they saw fit. While this may seem a risky idea at first, it allows me to track all the changes and edits and who makes them. Since one of the key characteristics of a wiki is the ability to "roll back" any change to any point in time, I was able to accept multiple updates, which gave me market intelligence into what the members were thinking and in what direction they wanted the organization to go. After a while, I switched off the ability to edit and reverted the mission to the original, while a portion of the executive committee reviewed the edits to determine which (if any) suggestions would be incorporated.

The great opportunity with nonprofits lies in the general accountability members have to the organization. Unlike Wikipedia, which allows anyone to update a page without even being logged in, most associations opt for a more conservative approach whereby the wiki can be edited only by someone who is not just logged in but is logged in as an active member. Since everyone who is editing a page must be logged in as a member, there is much greater accountability, especially when you consider people who made edits have their name and potentially photo automatically attached to their latest edits. This extra accountability really helps enforce the quality of the content.

Purpose-Built Wikis

Generally, the broader the scope of your wiki, the more difficult and overwhelming it can be for your members to grasp. Can you imagine launching a Wikipedia for your industry where you try to build an encyclopedia for anything and everything about your industry or interest? It would be difficult at best. A user group's product documentation wiki is a good example of trying to narrow the scope a little, but even this can be overwhelming at first. Normally, you'd need to at least start the project using staff resources to put together a basic structure—perhaps a home page and table of contents—before asking members to engage.

The glossary of terms wiki idea is a great example of a true purpose-built wiki with a narrow scope. In this example, each entry represents a single phrase, term, or acronym. For each entry there is just one page of content, which can be easily updated by anyone. When updating an entry, the user is presented with a WYSIWYG editor so there is no need to understand any of the more complex wiki syntax. This is an important factor if you want to engage the more tech-challenged members.

A good purpose-built wiki should have a status feature. Members are hesitant to edit something if they think they could be criticized for a mistake. For example, if a member sees a simple typo, they are reluctant to fix it because they know it will then show that they last updated it, even though they may have just fixed a typo. The perception is that they are responsible for the entire entry. Providing some sort of simple status functionality is more inviting to members. For example, if I want to add a new entry but don't have the time to go into too much detail, I might add:

Term: Social Media

Description:
Social media is a collaborative environment where users can view and share content.

Status: Description needs more detail.

When someone else comes along, they might see this and click on edit and change to the following:

Term: Social Media

Description:
Popularized by websites such as YouTube.com, Facebook.com, MySpace.com, Flickr.com, etc., Social Media is all about user-generated content (UGC) where anyone and everyone is invited to upload files such as videos and podcasts as well as more traditional files like Word or Excel into an environment that is typically open (can be viewed by anyone) and also allows people to comment, rate, and review the shared information.

Status: Someone confirm this is accurate.

Providing a user-friendly "Status" saves users from putting their reputations on the line by implying (by omission of a status to say otherwise) that the entry is perfect when indeed they may know it is far from it.

Other Document Collaboration Options

Wikis work extremely well with online web-based content but not so well for more traditional file-based collaboration. File-based collaboration is where someone downloads and opens a file, such as Word or Excel, and makes changes to that document for someone else to review and edit.

The problem with this type of collaboration option is that only one person can edit a document at a time. If I am reviewing a draft chapter of a publication in Word, and I download it and edit it, what happens when another committee member is updating the same chapter at the same time? We both eventually upload the document back to the online holding area and one of us will overwrite the changes of the other. A number of software vendors have attempted to provide a solution to this problem.

Google and Microsoft are probably the leaders in this area. Google Docs is an online area that allows you to collaborate on file-based documents with simple check-in and check-out functionality. The downside of this is that it does not integrate into your main database and there is no single sign on (SSO), so members must create a username and password. Microsoft has launched SharePoint, a product that allows you to do something similar. You can log into a website, be authenticated, and then check out a document. When someone else arrives to check it out, they are told that the document is already checked out by another user, but they can see a read-only version in the meantime. There are pros and cons to both solutions, and neither is ideal.

In 2005, when I was the CIO of the Risk & Insurance Management Society, Inc. (RIMS), I decided to use SharePoint. The RIMS Membership & Chapter Services committee was tasked with updating a book that had not been revised in about 10 years. The SharePoint environment was set up and the check-in/out functionality was verified by a couple of the committee members and all seemed to work well. We launched it to the entire committee with a project plan detailing which sub-groups would be editing or reviewing which chapters. We didn't account for the fact that some of the committee members were using much older versions of Word. This meant the checkout functionality wasn't working and resulted in the overwriting of previously uploaded versions. Entire sections went out of sync. This example demonstrates how external variables can hinder the goal in more complex collaborative environments.

Keep It Simple

In many areas of this book I talk about the importance of semantics. The truth is that many of our members, donors, and other constituents are intimidated by technology. When introducing the concept of collaborative editing, think carefully about your messaging. For example, if you email your members, asking them to help update your new "Wiki Glossary," it may immediately be perceived as intimidating by some. Depending on your demographic, it may be wise to change your messaging to something along the lines of:

> Help us update our online industry glossary by finding three terms that interest you and then simply click on edit to make any changes you think appropriate.

Notice how the word wiki was not even mentioned? Of course, after they have updated, you can always send them an email saying, "Thank you for updating the wiki glossary," as a subtle way of letting them know they have actually edited a wiki (whether they knew it or not).

Reference

1. http://en.wikipedia.org/wiki/Encyclopedia.

CHAPTER 3

Listening with the Social Web

Traditionally, communications or marketing people have always made a point of trying to monitor what is being said about their brand. This could involve subscribing to news services and industry-specific magazines or publications. Knowing what is being said about your organization is important for:

- Market intelligence
- Monitoring of your brand
- Trademark protection

Members and donors are more empowered than ever to voice their opinions about your organization using public forums. They can also post comments anonymously. Take Twitter as an example. It is a great way of getting immediate feedback about the products and services provided by your organization, actions taken by your organization, and new programs or services you are considering.

The traditional way of obtaining customer satisfaction feedback would have been via an annual survey or telemarketing and conference calling. That type of feedback is solicited, customers are responding to questions provided by you and your team. There are now a myriad of tools available for users to give their opinions, views, and thoughts anytime they desire, to whoever will listen. The benefit of this type of feedback is that it's unsolicited and driven by a motive or emotion. An action taken by your association has prompted someone (in addition to or instead of picking up the phone and calling you) to log into Twitter or Facebook and talk about it. Whether it is singing your praises about extraordinary actions taken or publicly defaming you for something you did or didn't do, they can tell whoever might be listening or searching for this information.

There are many new tools for monitoring online discussions. While this may sound like a daunting task, since it is yet another job to do, if you are strategic about how you do it, it should not take much time at all. In addition, the market intelligence you can gather may help avert a larger, more time-intensive crisis down the road. But monitoring is only one side of the equation. Listening is about more than just hearing what your audience is telling you; it is also about reacting and responding. The association needs to be nimble enough to respond. Associations that have to run every press release or public statement or comment by a committee of volunteers or a task force will not be able to take full advantage of the benefits these new media offer. To really make an impact, associations must empower staff to respond and ultimately become more nimble.

What to Listen/Search for

Every nonprofit is different in terms of what to search for, but here are some typical examples of what to listen for regarding your organization:

- Organization name
- Organization acronym
- Your competitors' names and acronyms
- Your products, services, and events
- Your competitors' products, services, and events
- Your brands/trademarks
- Industry terms
- Your CEO's name

How to Search

Before setting up alerts to help you listen to the web, you first need to test the search criteria. To do this, simply search for the relevant term. Using SNAMA as an example, the first thing I would do is go to Google and search for SNAMA. If the results displayed are the sort of results I would like to see in my alerts, then the search criteria are good. If not, then they need to be refined. For example, if I performed the same exercise for RIMS, the first search result would be for the Risk & Insurance Management Society, Inc. (the RIMS I am searching for), but most of the other results have to do with wheel rims and have no relevance. If I were to setup an alert for just RIMS, I would receive constant messages with non-relevant information. There are simple ways to refine your search. Here are just a few of the most obvious:

- Use quotes to search for a phrase, such as "social media." This would return results with the exact phrase "social media" rather than a page which contains the word "social" and somewhere else in the page "media."
- Use the minus sign to exclude anything with a specific word or phrase. Using the RIMS example, I would use: `RIMS -wheel`. This would exclude anything with the word "wheel" in the results.
- Use a combination of the above, for example:

```
RIMS "risk insurance" -wheel
```

Using the final example made every result relevant to my search. The problem with this is that it has now become such a specific search that I may not be alerted to something which falls slightly outside the search criteria. For example, if there is a risk management blog created about Firestone tires, it may well mention the word "wheel," which means I would not be alerted to it.

How to Listen

Many tools allow you to effectively listen to the web. Some follow the "push" method, sending you emails or text messages alerting you to new material, while others require you to go looking for the information. If you're a person who has difficulty managing the onslaught of email, you might prefer to visit several monitoring sites while sipping your coffee in the morning or winding down on a Friday afternoon. Be aware that the latter approach requires activity on your part, and you might miss something urgent if it is released in the middle of the day. Below is a sample of these tools.

The simplest and must-have listening devices are two alerting tools which use the "push" method, Google.com/alerts and Tweetbeep.com.

Google.com/alerts

Go to Google.com/alerts and set up alerts for your own name as a simple test of how this works. The screen should be self-explanatory, such as:

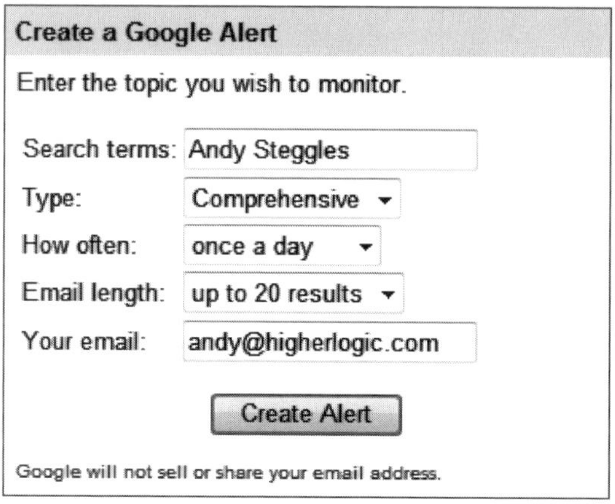

In the above example, I searched for my name without any quotes. This is because after testing the search in Google, I was satisfied with the relevance of the results. If I had not been, my next step would have been to test the search results for my name in quotes (exact phrase). Google will now deliver one email message per day with new search results containing Andy Steggles.

Tweetbeep.com

Tweetbeep.com is just like Google alerts except it is specifically for Twitter postings. This tool has been made a little simpler than Google because if you use their premium service you do not have to use things like minus signs. In this case, you would just enter the word you do not want included in "None of these words." Like Google Alerts, Tweetbeep allows you to set up the alert frequency. Another way to manage these push notifications is to set up a rule in your email program (known as a "rule" in Outlook, for example) to move these alerts to a folder in your inbox where you can read them when you're ready to focus on them. In Outlook, they will still show as new messages inside that folder, so you know you have received new alerts yet don't feel the pressure to read what's in your inbox at that very moment.

Some examples of tools you can set up to visit when you want to gather information using the "pull" method are:

HootSuite

HootSuite can show multiple Twitter feeds highlighting up to three keywords each. By watching your industry keywords, you can see what other people in your industry (members, potential members, key players, competitors) are discussing. By monitoring your association name (or acronym, since Twitter has a restrictive number of characters), you can see if there are tweets about your organization. You can also have a feed showing folks who re-tweet your message (more information about that later in the chapter on Twitter). The best part is that you can have *all three of those particular feeds showing on the same screen at the same time.*

Blog Search

Another useful thing to do when you start the listening process is a point-in-time search using both Google and the blog and news search engines to see how many results there are for your organization. The only purpose this will serve is that you have a rough idea of how many results there were prior to your social initiatives compared to various points in time after it. Using SNAMA as the example, I would use the following websites to do a search using the following criteria:

Search Term	Number of Results		
	Google google.com	**Google Blog Search google.com/ blogsearch**	**Google News google.com/news**
SNAMA*	737,000	17,064	63
SNAMA social	19,100	96	0
SNAMA association	12,600	56	1
Social Networking and Media Association*	156 million	1.1 million	494
"Social Networking and Media Association"	102,000	9	0

* Most results are not relevant and so the figures in this search don't really count for anything.

One final trick with searching is if you want to know the number of results but simultaneously want to exclude a specific website you can use the following:

```
SNAMA social -site:SNAMA.org
```

In the above example, the result showed me how many times the words "SNAMA" and "social" appeared in the search engines while excluding the entire SNAMA.org website.

By using the `site` parameter, we can include or exclude anything from a specific domain which includes any sub-domains. In other words, it has removed any page which is found on www.SNAMA.org and also careers.SNAMA.org (the SNAMA community managers' job bank).

Tip: Do a regular search for your site to see how many pages are indexed from your website. As your social initiatives grow, so should the number of indexed pages (assuming not all are members only). It should be part of your social networking strategy to record this information so you can track and compare over time. For instance, if your organization is attempting to standardize a term, record the search results over time to prove the effectiveness of your marketing and public relations efforts. Or if you have access to analytical software that tracks the areas of the world your search hits are coming from, you can show the activity in that area over time, attributing success (or failure) to costly travel budgets or other campaigns.

When I do a search for just `site:SNAMA.org`, there are 285 pages. Note, the result for the search `site:snama.org` (in lower case) is the same since I have used Google webmaster tools to let Google know they are both the same site. See Chapter 9 on search engines for more information about this.

Other search engines to listen through are:

- Yahoo.com (Yahoo tends to index anything but is selective about what it displays.)
- Ask.com (a new but emerging search engine)
- Bing.com (a recent replacement to Microsoft Search)
- Technorati.com (one of the most well-known blog search engines)
- Digg.com (a news referral and rating website)
- Delicious.com (a social bookmarking website, good to monitor how many people are bookmarking pages in your website)

Really Simple Syndication (RSS)

Another simple way to listen to the web is to do various searches and then take the RSS feed from the search results and plug them into your RSS aggregator, iGoogle.com being a great example of this. Try searching for your name at search.twitter.com and then when you see the results, click on the RSS icon, copy the URL and then add it to your new iGoogle.com home page (create an account if you don't have one). You should then see the results of that search on your iGoogle.com home page in real time.

Advanced Listening Tools

What if your brand is too big to listen to using the most basic and mostly free listening techniques and tools? What happens if it is simply impossible to keep up and read all the blogs/comments and reviews that refer to your brand or your industry at large? Then you should start testing various tools to see if they might fit your needs. Larger organizations hire for-profit agencies to act as their ears and provide listening packages. I recommend you manage this task yourself, at least initially, so you become fully aware of the capabilities and will be able to know what to expect from your vendor.

Examples of Advanced Listening Tools

Alterian SM2 (socialmedia.alterian.com)

Monitors the number of new search results by day

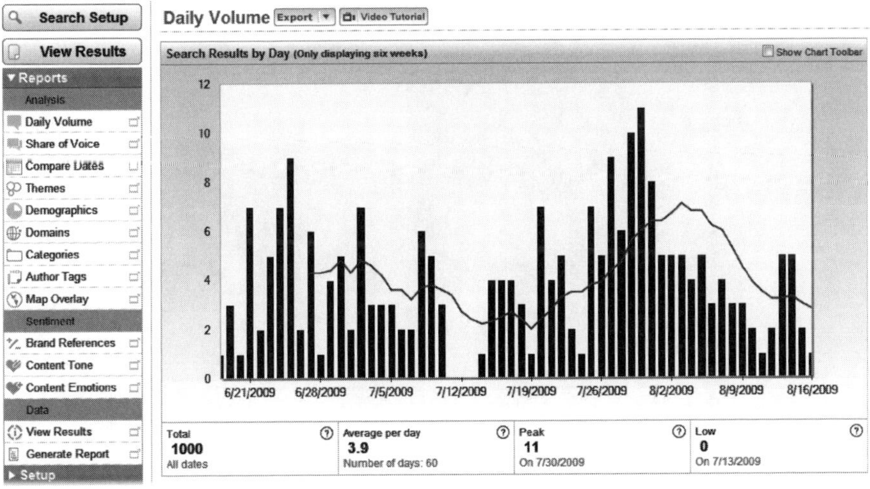

Tells which media the various hits have been found on

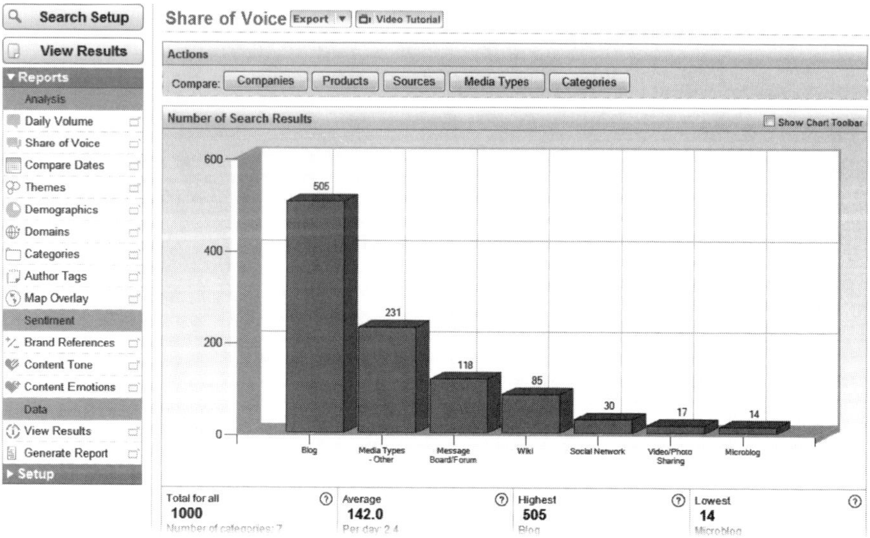

The two reports I find most interesting are the ones that tell you the sentiment and tone of the web:

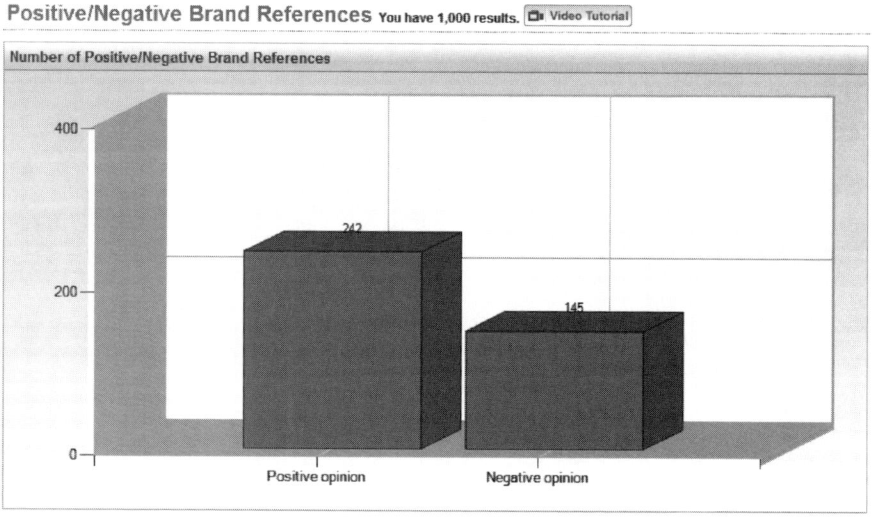

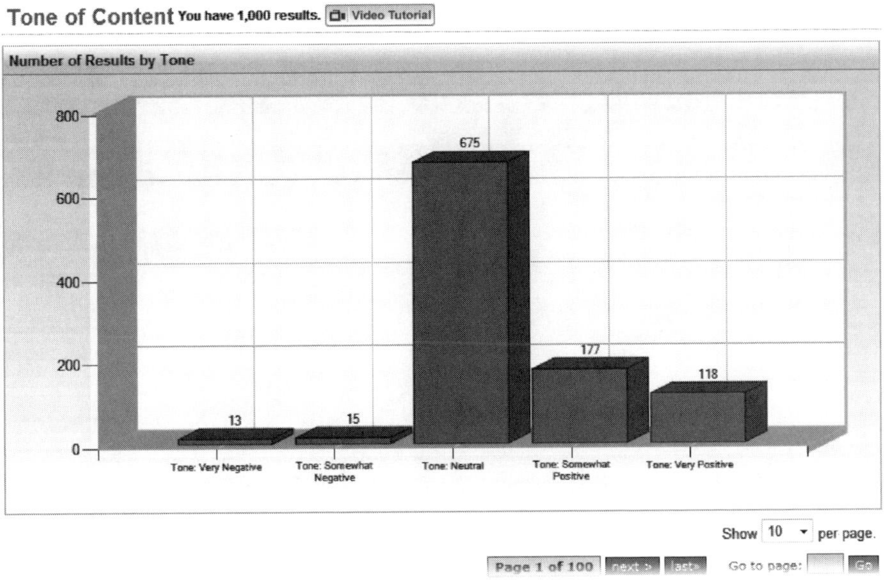

Other website tools to look at include:

- http://www.compete.com
- http://www.comscore.com
- http://www.alexa.com

Some of the above sites serve a more specific purpose. For example, in the list of listening objectives above, we mentioned competitors. If you have a competitor and want to compare how you are performing against that competitor, consider a report like the following from compete.com:

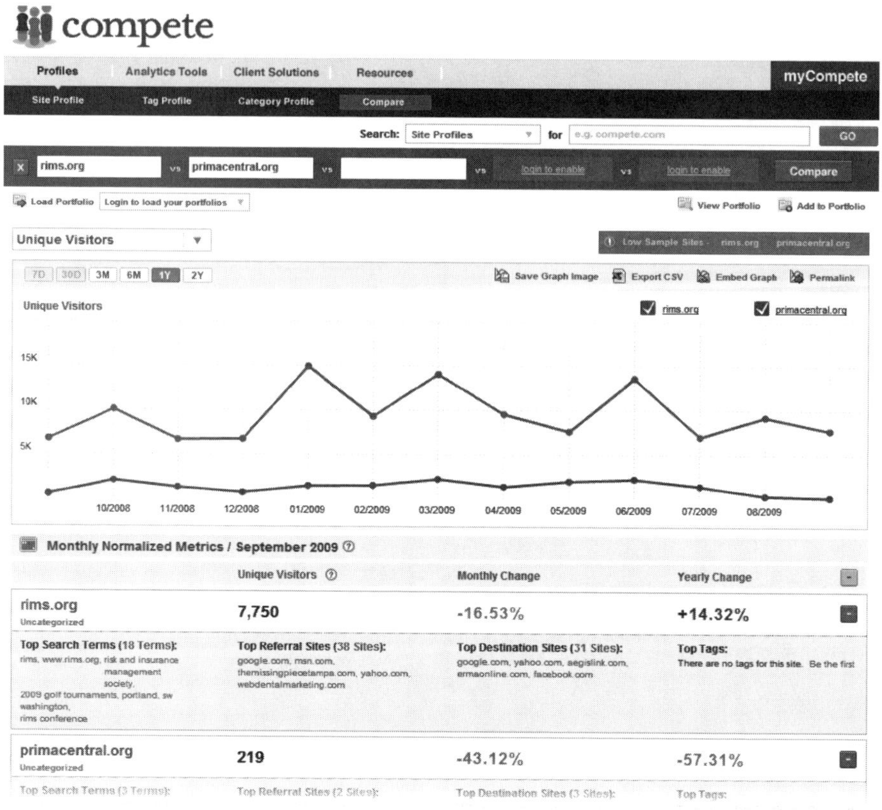

Establish Yourself

Blogging etiquette was discussed in a previous chapter. As someone who is listening and monitoring the brand of your organization, even if you do not blog, you should get to know the bloggers. Many bloggers hold social influence within your sphere and establishing a relationship with them can be a good thing. It may be very useful when you next want to launch a product or service and part of your marketing strategy is to invite bloggers to test drive the new proverbial vehicle. Consider giving the most popular bloggers within your industry a free registration to your annual conference or other prominent events—just as you might for more traditional press contacts.

As you start receiving alerts for the various key phrases you have set up, you will start to be drawn to many of the same bloggers over and again. Start to put together your own A-list of industry bloggers, and then take time to subscribe to them and comment and rate. If you have your own blog, instead of commenting on their blog, trying using a backlink from your blog.

Blogs are not the only things to which you should be responding. When monitoring Twitter, create another A-list and occasionally re-tweet (see Chapter 5 about Twitter) what they post if you find it worthy. This will likely prompt them to monitor you, and then when you tweet about a new service or product, they may re-tweet about it, thus generating more exposure for your organization.

When using public social networking sites, such as Facebook or LinkedIn, which allow users to form groups or create "pages," find and join other groups that are likely to attract prospective and current members. Be sure to subscribe to these groups so you are alerted when discussion topics are posted or comments are made. This is another way to be listening to what is going on and perhaps get a proactive edge in discussing new issues or initiatives.

Personal Brand

Most of this listening section focuses on the organization. Be sure you take a similar approach to monitor your own identity and brand. Set up alerts for your own name and, if necessary, narrow the results by location or something else closely related to your professional brand.

Remember: The conversation is happening whether you're listening to it or not.

CHAPTER 4

Facebook, LinkedIn, and Other Outposts

By Lindy Dreyer and Maddie Grant, CAE

When you say "social networking," the first thing most people think of are popular public sites like Facebook, MySpace, LinkedIn, Twitter, and others. These are outposts—public social spaces where an organization can have a social media presence within large existing communities and without owning the site. Any public site where people "socialize" around specific content can be an outpost. There are many kinds of outposts: social networks like Facebook, LinkedIn, and MySpace; media sharing sites such as YouTube, Flickr, SlideShare, Ustream; microblogging sites like Twitter, Plurk; lifestreaming sites like FriendFeed; social bookmarking sites like Delicious, Digg, StumbleUpon; and even popular blogs and forums that are not expressly affiliated with your organization. The common denominators for all these sites are that they are open to anyone who wants to participate and they enable social interaction.

Consider the fact that Facebook added more than 100 million users in just six months;[1] that every minute, more than 20 hours of video is uploaded to YouTube;[2] that a new member joins LinkedIn approximately every second.[3] With a simple search on any of these networks, you'll be able to see if groups are forming around your industry, if your most visible members are there, and even if a group has already started using the name of your organization. People who regularly use these sites—whether to share photos with their families or to connect professionally—are comfortable with the tool they've chosen. Some are early adopters who will happily join and use a number of different sites. Others will stick to what they know. From a marketing and community-building perspective, outposts pose an interesting opportunity to engage with members where they are already hanging out online.

This is the crux of why outposts are important: If you have something with enough value that people want to socialize around it and create their own microcommunities, it's crucial to be able to 1) find these self-formed communities and 2) reach out to them to make them part of your overall social media strategy without necessarily taking them over.

Official Versus Unofficial Outposts

Associations need to be prepared to engage with two different types of outposts—official outposts and unofficial outposts. Official outposts are built by organizations that deliberately engage stakeholders on a pubic site. This might take any number of forms: a page on Facebook, a group on LinkedIn or Flickr, a hashtag on Twitter, a channel on YouTube, and more. With an official outpost, an organization may have some administrative control of who can participate, what content is posted, and what content is removed. They have control over the logo. They might even have some guidelines in place to help shape the conversations that happen in their space. With official outposts, it is important to create a valuable space in which the participants have some stake in the success of the group. If an organization tries to exert unwelcome control over the group, it is both easy and common for the group members who feel slighted to go off and form their own group.

Unofficial outposts are self-formed groups that the organization is not involved in creating or managing. For associations, unofficial outposts are a frequent phenomenon, as members and industry stakeholders find one another in public social spaces and begin gathering there. Unofficial outposts are a great opportunity for associations that are just getting into social media. If your members are already gathering, they have done much of the work of community building for you. Simply by joining, getting to know the group administrators, and offering to help in small ways, you can take advantage of this head start. Many associations find unofficial outposts that are formed using the association's name, acronym, or logo. Often these groups welcome involvement from the association. It is important to approach these groups from a position of trust and mutual respect, as they are likely your biggest fans.

Susan Kistler, executive director for the American Evaluation Association (AEA) notes both the benefits and challenges of unofficial outposts. "We began looking at LinkedIn primarily because we were receiving complaints from members trying to join a group with the association's name on it and not being responded to in a timely manner. As we learned more, a cross-reference of our membership database with the LinkedIn database—quickly accomplished through a tool on the LinkedIn site—showed that over half of our members had profiles on LinkedIn. The need to maintain positive member relations and our commitment to go where our members already are factored heavily into our decision to strengthen our presence on LinkedIn. Working with the existing group owners, who were enthusiastic members but did not have the time or resources needed to administer or grow the community, we collaboratively decided to have AEA take over administrative control. We retained the pre-existing owners as facilitators with administrative rights, and added review of the site as part of the daily staff function to ensure that it was spam-free and that requests to join were rapidly approved. As we let our members know of the LinkedIn outpost, its membership grew from fewer than 150 to more than 2,000 in nine months."

Strategies for Using Outposts

There are as many strategies for using outposts as there are associations using them. Here are a few strategies that associations have used effectively.

Finding and Monitoring Outposts

The first step in using outposts to build community is knowing where they are. Listening and monitoring the social web for mentions of your organization and relevant industry keywords or names will help you find out where people are talking about you. Google Alerts can pull in news and blog mentions, and every social site has search capabilities for running keyword searches. There are also tools such as Addict-o-Matic (http://addictomatic.com) and How Sociable (www.howsociable.com) that can be used to look across multiple social networking sites for keyword mentions. Many public social networks allow you to import email lists (but remember to check that your email privacy policies allow you to use the email addresses of members this way!) to see if the organization's members are already there and are, therefore, potentially likely to be interested in interacting with the organization in those spaces.

Outposts as Individuals

Once you are aware of relevant groups in a few key outposts or enough members in those outposts to create a group if one doesn't already exist, you can start to participate in those groups as individual staff members. Social media is about individuals, and building relationships between staff and stakeholders is one key to being able to capitalize on brand-building later. Often, you will need to make those personal connections first—by allowing your staff to "friend" stakeholders on Facebook, invite colleagues to connect on LinkedIn, follow relevant people on Twitter—before you start inviting them to join your association's group or fan page or share your content. In other words, you are leveraging the latent social capital that your staff has built with members and other industry stakeholders to help grow and bind your online community. Be sure to provide guidelines for staff contributions to outposts that align with your association's culture and encourage professional, responsible, and transparent sharing.

> ***Resource!***
> Laurel Papworth has compiled an extensive list of social media staff guidelines and examples on her blog. Focusing on "the business of social media, online communities, and social networks," Papworth regularly provides insight into social media issues. See http://bit.ly/papworth.

Outposts for Branding

The key to protecting your brand in outposts is to make your official outpost larger and more robust—and thus easier to find in searches and through friends' connections. For organizations with chapters and components, an outpost strategy should include connections with all those groups. You might choose to join the group, connect with the administrators, cross-promote content, share logos, and more. National organizations may choose to make a list of all the smaller, more tightly bonded local and topic-related groups to make them easier for other members to find and join after connecting with the main, official group. You may also choose to reach out to unofficial groups—especially those using your name, acronym, or logo—and see if there's a way to help those groups be clear about their relationship to your organization.

Outposts As a Testing Ground

Before jumping in whole hog and spending time and resources building an internal network, many organizations start by experimenting in outposts as a way of building community, understanding the social actions your community prefers, and building your organizational capacity to manage the community. While your own home base website or social network will doubtless offer many advantages to any single public outpost—especially from a content and data perspective—there is still a lot to be learned from this type of experimentation, especially in the early stages of building community online.

Marketing Through Outposts

Outposts offer two types of marketing opportunities. You can concentrate on deliberate word-of-mouth marketing, which focuses on making it easy and worthwhile for your community to share your information among themselves. This is especially effective with events, small and large, as people begin registering and reaching out to see who else in their network is planning to go. Strong outposts also give you the option of running a social media campaign. This can be something simple, like a discount only for community members. Or it can be more complex, sometimes involving third party widgets or applications. Either way, the key to both word-of-mouth and campaign-based marketing is a strong, thriving, value-driven community that cares about your organization's issues. Without that, you risk being perceived as a spammer, and you will lose the loyalty of your stakeholders.

Feeding Your Home Base

For associations that have social spaces on their own website—comments and reviews on web pages, a blog, or even a full white-label social network—outposts are essential. There are many ways to cross-promote your home base to outposts and vice versa, ranging from simple sharing buttons to more full-featured integrations with another site's Application

Programming Interface (API). If your organization has a well-established Facebook page, for example, you may want to look into a close integration using Facebook Connect. Facebook, LinkedIn, Twitter, and many other outposts have open APIs that enable many types of interaction between sites. Thinking beyond the tools, the relationships you develop in outposts will give you a better understanding of the value your home base can offer that goes beyond what is already happening. You will also be able to identify member champions who can help promote your home base.

> ***Warning!***
> Be careful when you use automation to integrate across outposts. Since each outpost has a different culture and technical specifications, automation runs the risk of posting content that may be viewed as thoughtless (truncated twitter posts) to inappropriate (overly informal content fed from Facebook to LinkedIn).

Thirteen Steps for Building an Outpost Presence

1. Identify your objectives for entering into the social media space. Why are you willing to invest time and resources into such an endeavor?

2. Learn about each outpost site and its culture and contributors. Consider which ones align most closely with your mission, membership, and the image that you wish to convey.

3. Start by listening. Go to each outpost site (Twitter, Facebook, LinkedIn, for example) and run a search for relevant keywords.

4. "Friend" any known connections. Most sites allow you to search your email for connections that are already on the sites.

5. Join relevant unofficial groups and pay attention to what's happening inside them.

6. Use tools on each site to identify the extent of your membership base's participation on the site and weigh this information as part of your decision to invest resources.

7. Identify gaps in the value provided in those unofficial groups. It may not be necessary to have your own official group if there is a lot of good activity already happening and you can reach out and offer assistance (like a link to your website and a proper "fan of" logo).

8. Plant your flag. If there is no official group, but your members are asking for one, start one.
9. Invite all your relevant connections to your group. Tell people about your outpost presence.
10. Start providing good content to both unofficial and official groups. Tread lightly and don't spam, but as a member of a group you are able (and expected) to join the conversation.
11. Set up feeds to feed good blog content to your outposts.
12. Tie your accounts or groups to face-to-face events; it provides a great reason for people to connect around your content.
13. Interlink everything. Promote all your activity in all your outposts and on your home base website.

> ***Tip!***
> Make it easy for people to find and join your outposts by placing direct links on your association's homepage. Thomas Bohn noted via an ASAE LinkedIn Discussion, "Adding logos with links to our pages has dramatically improved the number of members who are LinkedIn to us!" You can see them at
> http://www.iappnet.org
> http://bit.ly/thomasbohn

Feeding Content into Outposts

Most organizations are already creating more than enough content to feed their outposts. What is needed is a strong content plan to organize and repurpose that content. Every good plan starts with an inventory—a list of content the organization already produces for the home base website. You might have white papers, articles, videos, news announcements, and more. The inventory should also list the department that produces the content, who is responsible for it, and how frequently it appears. Once you have the inventory, the trick is to repurpose the best content into bite-size chunks that are suitable for feeding your outposts.

One of the simplest ways to repurpose content is to use a Content Management System (CMS) or a blog platform like Wordpress, which inherently supports RSS feeds and sharing to social sites like Facebook and Twitter. For example, you can create one blog post that summarizes a popular article from your association magazine, with a link to the full article. Another blog post might embed a YouTube video of members summarizing what they learned at your conference. You can take the RSS feed from the blog and use it to automatically push those two posts to your Facebook fans, LinkedIn group members, and Twitter followers.

One rule for managing outposts is that they need regular feeding. An outpost with low activity will wither and die quickly. For some outposts, like a group formed around an event, a finite lifespan is fine. But for your main official outposts, care and feeding is an ongoing effort. The attention span of the social web is short—a good content plan will help ensure there is always something new to share.

Pushing Content Out of Outposts

Many outposts produce content on their own. An association blog will have blog entries, and Twitter feeds will have ongoing updates. One way to encourage use of this content is to ensure that it may be accessed not only via the outpost itself but through those media with which your members are most familiar. For many associations, this will be via email and/or association publications such as newsletters. Strategies for success here include reformatting content as needed and regularly referencing and linking to your social media content in traditional media channels to encourage use.

> ***Tip!***
> Running an RSS feed through Feedburner and then configuring Feedburner to allow subscription via email will allow you to monitor subscription volume as well as facilitate email-based access to the content.

Getting a Handle on Outposts

Feeding content into your outposts and pushing content out of outposts are just half of the equation. Using outposts for two-way interaction and building your community doesn't happen by itself, despite the inherently organic nature of social media and social spaces. Managing outposts takes staff time and resources, even when the tool itself is free to use. There are things you can do as an organization to build the capacity to handle outposts efficiently and effectively.

1. Track Both Official and Unofficial Outposts

Start a spreadsheet that tracks some basic information: outpost URL, descriptive name of the outpost, administrator name and email, and audience size to start. For unofficial outposts, also include the staff member who is most closely connected to that outpost through membership in the outpost, monitoring the space, or a close relationship with the administrator.

2. Build Relationships between Administrators and among Outposts

Depending on your organization, you may have multiple people with administrative rights to different outposts. Give them a way to coordinate efforts. There are many easy-to-use applications that connect Facebook and Twitter content, for example, or that use site feeds to automate some types of posts to outposts. You might also reach out to administrators of unofficial outposts to invite them to collaborate as well.

3. Define a Framework for All Staff to Participate

Organizations that are clear about expectations and boundaries with social media are positioning themselves to use outposts more efficiently in the future. A good framework will define policies for employees using social media, moderation rules for individual outposts, workflows for posting in official spaces, and a path for getting new ideas for using social media approved and implemented.

Managing Risks Associated with Outposts

Managing outposts, like any web presence, requires some level of risk tolerance and risk management. Some of the most serious risks relate to reputation management, branding, and intellectual property. Your members may also have risks associated with antitrust and other legal considerations. (See Chapter 7.) Many of the risks extend to your organization regardless of whether you are actively engaged in organizing official outposts. When you're creating your strategy for social media, assessing the risks to your organization is a useful exercise.

Ways to Move Beyond the Risks

Organized Monitoring

Setting up an organized means of monitoring outposts is a good first step. This way you'll be aware of conversations that are happening, and be better prepared to respond if necessary.

Policies

Your staff and key volunteers can benefit from a set of guidelines for the best ways to use social media—both personally for keeping private information private and professionally for promoting the organization.

Education

Make sure your staff understands what you are trying to achieve and the risks that may be involved. Social media snafus can be prevented through education about etiquette and laws governing social media.

User Agreements and Moderation

All social sites have their own terms of use governing all users, including your organization. Get to know them. And for official outposts, you can post a link to your own terms of use or user agreement. In that, you might state your moderation policy for the group and reminders about legal issues like copyright and antitrust. Having reasonable policies in plain English helps you create a safe space for your employees and stakeholders to operate.

Ask for Help

Your outpost communities can be self-regulating, too, and often someone in the community will flag administrators about something that warrants removal.

Group or Fan Page and Other Burning Questions

Facebook group or fan page? Twitter account or hashtag? LinkedIn free or premium? YouTube channel or tag? These are all common questions. Unfortunately, there is no easy answer. All these platforms are constantly changing, so what works best one day might be replaced by some new feature later. Things change so quickly that even by the time this book is published, any "best practices" we print could already need to be updated. Here's our current advice:

- Worry less about the features and more about the people. Where are your members? What aligns with your culture?
- Whatever you choose, start small and good, and give it time to develop.
- Subscribe to the blog for the tool you're using so you'll hear about changes first. (http://blog.facebook.com; http://blog.linkedin.com; http://blog.flickr.net/en; http://blog.twitter.com; http://youtube-global.blogspot.com)

Measuring Return on Investment (ROI)

As with every social media project or experiment, organizations need to measure the right things, to know if the experiment is working. The right things, then, will depend on the objectives defined for that activity. If an organization is trying to attract younger members on Facebook, they will measure different things than if they are trying to improve the thought leadership status of the brand through an advocacy campaign on Twitter. All social sites have some level of reporting; however, the association industry as a whole is still trying to figure out how to measure engagement, influence, and social capital—things that power the viral nature of the social web. There is no magic bullet. No matter what you measure, set a baseline at the beginning and be sure to include anecdotal or qualitative evidence as part of the reporting process.

Proving ROI for your outpost activity will not be easy. Some companies have reported significant ROI—like DELL, which announced that they've converted more than $6.5 million in sales over two years from their work on Twitter[4]—but theirs is a much different business model than the association and nonprofit model. That said, if you set reasonable and measurable goals for yourself, you will see an impact from your work that you can share with your board and other association leaders. Some realistic goals might include:

- Gather email addresses from a LinkedIn group for prospective members and conference attendees. You might do a quarterly comparison of the LinkedIn members with your membership database and track the conversion rates for new emails from the outpost.
- Increase registration for eLearning programs. You might use a URL shortener like bit.ly to track click-throughs on your registration site from social spaces like Twitter.

- Drive web traffic to a publication site featuring advertisers. You might track referral sites on your web analytics dashboard to see which social spaces are driving traffic.
- Identify and engage early adopters who will champion a new white-label social network. When new users log in for the first time, you might ask them where they first heard about the new social network and include your outposts among the options.
- Build awareness (and search optimization) for a specific program or the association overall. You might track the number of mentions through Google Alerts or another more powerful buzz monitoring system, like Radian6, ScoutLabs, or Alterian SM2.

The Point

Outposts are important because your stakeholders are already there. When building a strategy for using outposts, consider official outposts that your organization manages as well as unofficial outposts that are created by members and other industry stakeholders. Feeding your official outposts is as simple as identifying and repurposing content you are already creating. Getting a handle on the two-way nature of outposts takes a greater, more organized effort. Your work will be more effective if you have good social media policies and education options in place for your staff and key volunteers. Risks are inherent in outposts, regardless of whether you are actually participating. Assessing your risks and managing them effectively is important for your outpost strategy, as is measurement. Proving ROI is not easy, but if you choose reasonable, measurable goals, you will have something to show for your work.

References

1. http://www.facebook.com/press/info.php?timeline.
2. http://www.youtube.com/t/fact_sheet.
3. http://press.linkedin.com/about.
4. http://www.fastcompany.com/blog/kit-eaton/technomix/twitter-really-works-makes-65-million-sales-dell.

CHAPTER 5

Associations Atwitter

By KiKi L'Italien

Tweet, tweet. On the face of it, Twitter seems silly. What could possibly be worth saying in 140 characters or less with the prompt, "What's happening?" As much as associations need to focus on communication strategies rather than the tools, discussing the unique niche that Twitter fills is necessary to any discussion about social media for organizations.

The Elements of Twitter

Twitter is a communication platform that allows people to post messages of up to 140 characters. It rewards the succinct and because of that, cuts through the excess to allow for fast, digestible bits of information.

Short and Sweet

One could communicate Ernest Hemingway's words from *The Sun Also Rises:*

> Then there was another thing. He had been reading W.H. Hudson. That sounds like an innocent occupation, but Cohn read and reread "The Purple Land." "The Purple Land" is a very sinister book if read too late in life. It recounts splendid imaginary amorous adventures of a perfect English gentleman in an intensely romantic land, the

scenery of which is very well described.
(233 characters)

– Ernest Hemingway. *The Sun Also Rises*. New York: Simon & Schuster, 1926.

Twitter-ized version:

> @Cohn read Hudson's The Purple Land. http://bit.ly/7O3Z24. Can you say, "midlife crisis"?
> (52 characters)

Twitter has a simple structure. You participate using your alias, a user name preceded by the "@" symbol. For example, my Twitter alias is @kikilitalien and Andy Steggles' alias is @asteggles. Updates are called "tweets" on Twitter. When you are responding to a tweet, you reference the originator of the post. For example:

> Thank you @kikilitalien for sharing the link to Acronym.

Possibly even more important than establishing your own presence on Twitter is identifying people or groups to follow who are already using the platform. When you follow someone on Twitter, it simply means you choose to read their tweets. There are a number of ways you can find interesting people to follow, including using Monitter.com and Twellow.com.

These tools will allow you to find people to follow based on keywords and interests or people connected to you already using their individual usernames.

The Importance of Listening

Mindful listening is important in Twitter. With a Twitter user name and a group of interesting people and groups to follow, associations can choose to use Twitter primarily as another broadcasting tool or as a vehicle to engage with their members and potential members.

Every association should monitor Twitter. Why? To be able to receive helpful feedback from online communities already discussing your association, to quickly respond to public relations and customer service issues, or to keep track of industry keywords important to your organization.

There are free websites that allow you to choose keywords to monitor on Twitter. Monitter is one such website that tracks a set of keywords and allows you to watch what people are saying. Social Oomph is another.

To realize the value in monitoring Twitter, start with three keywords that you want to track, and type them into the columns. In Monitter, you can even change your search preference, to see what's being talked about in a particular area (by zip code).

Quickly you will likely see a stream of tweets coming in on topics related to your keyword. Not all of them will be an ideal match, but you will likely run across an article or resource of some kind that you would not have found otherwise.

Another important technique used to listen is the hashtag.

What Is a Hashtag?

A hashtag is a way for people to search for tweets that have a common topic. Hashtags allow Twitter users to discuss topics in real time and to collect those posts later for review. The hashtag comes in especially handy for events because it establishes an easy online "backchannel" for participants and can attract to the conversation people who may not be familiar with your association.

For example, the upcoming Apple Growers Convention may send their membership news about the convention with a note to follow #AGC2010 to get the latest updates about the meeting on Twitter. Every time a person then sends a tweet about the meeting using the hashtag #AGC2010, everyone following that hashtag will see the message.

In addition, one may optionally reserve a hashtag using a number of free sites. Although, it should be noted that reserving a hashtag on one of these sites does not necessarily mean no one else will use it for something completely different. The value of reserving a hashtag announces to the world your intentions to use it even if you are not already. While you can't enforce it, it will reduce the likelihood that someone else will use it.

Identify, Publish, and Use Your Hashtag

Search on Twitter.com (http://search.twitter.com) for the hashtag you think you want to use, or browse the directory at Hashtags.org. Is the hashtag already in use for another purpose? If so, it is generally best to avoid confusion by choosing a different one. If the hashtag was used only a few times or used by individuals rather than organizations, then you might be able to use the hashtag anyway.

Hashtag dictionary websites are not directly affiliated with Twitter, so many Twitter users don't know these dictionary sites exist. Others may not think to check these sites when selecting a new hashtag. Still, listing your new hashtag with these sites can help to formalize your usage of that tag and acts as a service to those perceptive Twitter users who do look up unfamiliar hashtags. The following are five popular sites where you can list and define your new hashtag:

1. WhatTheHashtag.com
2. HashDictionary.com
3. Tagalus.com
4. Tagdef.com
5. Tagref.com

Use the hashtag regularly and encourage your staff and members to use it as well. Ideally, the hashtag will be strongly associated with your organization or event.

Conversation Tracking

How you use Twitter is up to you, but it's good practice to monitor the Twitter conversation as part of your organization's due diligence.

Once you understand how Twitter can play a role in customer service, the next step should center on conversation tracking. What are people already saying about you? Have people misinterpreted your latest bylaws change? What about the good things they say? Track all the possible keywords that are related to your industry, like the names of your scholarships, meetings, events, or any nickname your company may have. (Note: While this section focuses specifically on Twitter, see Chapter 3 for a deeper understanding of how to listen more holistically.) No other medium gets you inside an association or brand quite like Twitter. It fills a need for fast, shorthand communication. Quick bites of information easily digested and shared, Twitter is a game changer because of its malleability for communication, including:

- Customer Service and Brand Management
- Breaking News and Announcements
- Member Engagement
- Special Events

Customer Service and Brand Management

Customer service opportunities abound in Twitter and there is a seemingly endless list of examples to help explain why an association should use a microblogging tool. Today, good member service includes monitoring and sometimes responding to conversations about the association or the industry in a timely manner—and a "timely manner" is a very short span of time when dealing with online media.

An Ideal Customer Service Platform

Before calling the association's board into a meeting and exclaiming your organization must use Twitter, you need to understand why Twitter and customer service is such a successful pairing. Here is how the basic tenants of good customer service relate to Twitter:

Problem Resolution

The main goal of member service is to help people resolve issues. While phone conversations can help solve problems, wait times do not. Twitter is a lightning-fast platform that can help sift through and solve problems quickly. If it is a small issue, a single tweet may be enough. For a more complex problem, the association can initiate a deeper conversation with the member. Twitter management tools, like Co-Tweet, may be used to assign tweets to colleagues for faster response and to track when those tweets are addressed.

Positive Brand Image

Great customer service is shared. People will talk about great service, and this can lead to more sales and more attention. Twitter is one of the most viral platforms around, which can make one happy member into an international story.

Proper Staffing
If the team does not buy into the notion of helping the member, the result will be sub-par assistance. Twitter is not only a more interesting platform than phone or email, but gives staff a better picture of their impact on others.

Cost Efficiency
Customer service via Twitter often takes less time and a lot less money than a dedicated call center. With Twitter, it is necessary to be short and to the point, which reduces the time needed to solve each problem.

Make Members Aware of Your Presence

Watching a conversation gives you a good idea of your association's reputation and standing in social media and elsewhere, but it is a passive approach. Great member service is active. To get started, make your Twitter presence known. Ask users to follow you on Twitter, prominently place a button on your website and advertise that you are trying to engage with your members in problem resolution via social media. Member service on Twitter will not work if nobody knows where to find you.

Respond Clearly and Quickly

The key to great member service is the speed and quality of your response. When you find people complaining about an issue, reply to them using their @alias, asking if you can help. Do not take an arrogant tone and do not tell them that they screwed up. Ask if they would like you to intervene and then provide them with the information they need. This is why training in social media is critical for the entire staff of your organization.

If a problem is sensitive, the member is extraordinarily upset, or you want to get in contact with a member fast, either try to direct message them or give them a fast way to contact you, like a special email address or even a personal phone number. Let them know you are there to help and go with them step-by-step. To direct message someone, precede the message with the letter D followed by a space and their alias. For example:

D @asteggles Andy, can you give me your tel num so I can call about this

Simply replying with the person's alias is the best (this is referred to as @replies) as this is public and there are no restrictions on who you can reply to and it provides a public and transparent face to your member service. Others can see what you are doing, which can help reassure members or even solve problems they were going to ask you about, saving you additional time.

Be Human

Twitter is a conversational platform, and people like to talk to people, so take time to chat as well. Twitter is an opportunity to build an image and identity for your association, so talking with members about the area, what cool things your organization has done, or tweeting a success story gives people many reasons to follow what you say.

Even if you are using software or a website to manage Twitter member service, it needs to be supplemented with personal conversations. Autopilot Tweet is software that makes it easy for purchasers to make multiple accounts, find new people to follow, and schedule tweets. It advertises that it will increase your followers, but it takes more than followers to make your Twitter existence important. Unless they understand your Twitter alias to be used for breaking news only, people will tune out your messages if you take out the human touch.

While software like Autopilot Tweet and websites like socialoomph.com can make it easier for users to manage time spent on social media, you risk automating everything to the point of removing the value of the experience.

Be Honest

Most of all, when you are conducting member service and member relationship management, you need to be forthcoming. It is easier than ever for your members to research whether you are telling the truth. If you are not telling the truth, they will punish you by mobilizing and making their anger heard.

Despite this warning, the benefits to your brand and your members by using Twitter as a member service platform are immense. The American

Red Cross, The American Academy of Physician's Assistants, Comcast, Dell, Southwest Airlines, Ford, Starbucks, and many more organizations have been successful in promoting a positive brand image and solving problems with less cost than phone or email service. Twitter and social media are helping redefine customer service.

Breaking News and Announcements

It is easy to forget the weight words carry and the power of brevity. Twitter's limited character count forces concise posts about even the most complex of topics. This short, but to-the-point conversation helps mobilize people in a way we are only beginning to understand.

Research in the Clouds

In December 2009, the Defense Advanced Research Projects Agency (DARPA) kicked off a contest asking teams to locate the longitudes and latitudes of 10 red weather balloons positioned in stationary locations across the continental United States. Although the contest was officially open for seven days, it only took nine hours for the team from MIT to locate all 10 balloons, winning the competition and $40,000 in prize money.

The goal of the project was not to see who could answer the question, but how. More specifically, "the roles the internet and social networking play in the timely communication, wide-area team-building, and urgent mobilization required to solve broad-scope, time-critical problems." (DARPA, 2009, http://www.darpa.mil/events.html)

In the MIT team's case, it looks like they had a solid information infrastructure set up before the contest. Potential team members could sign up to join the team from the group's website and then invite friends using their own identifiable link. The tracking link makes it easy for the team to distribute the winning funds to not just the people that identified a balloon but the person who invited them to join the team in the first place.

Momentous Tweets

Following are some momentous tweets, showing how remarkable Twitter can be at breaking news and exchanging information.

There's a plane in the Hudson.

"There's a plane in the Hudson. Im on the ferry going to pick up the people. Crazy (@jkrums)" released the first image of the Hudson River plane crash on Twitter. If any one event opened the eyes to the media and the public about the power of quickly communicating real time events—even in fewer than 140 characters—it's the Hudson plane crash Twitter story. This was a turning point for the relationship of news, journalism, and Twitter.

Are you ready to celebrate?

"Well, get ready: We have ICE!!!!! Yes, ICE, *WATER ICE* on Mars! W00t!!! Best day ever!! (@MarsPhoenix)" When ice was found on Mars, the news was broken by the Twitter account of the Mars Phoenix Lander.

Arrested

"Arrested (@jamesbuck)" On April 10, 2008, James Karl Buck and his translator were arrested by the Egyptian police while covering an anti-government protest. Buck, a grad student from Berkeley, was able to tweet one word while being taken away by Egyptian authorities: "Arrested." This one update sparked his friends and followers into action, eventually leading to his university's hiring a lawyer on his behalf and his release a day later, proof that a single word can mobilize people and change the course of events.

Gosh, magntude7.8

"Gosh, magntude7.8… God Bless…http://earthquake.usgs.gov/… (@dtan)" It can take hours to write a good news article or blog post, 30 minutes to write a breaking news article, and even five minutes to write a couple lines to break the story. With status updates, it takes a matter of seconds. This has enabled Twitter to break news even before the news stations.

The Status Update

The status update fundamentally influenced how news is broken and tracked by the public today. As social media grows more and more popular, the status update will be central in how our culture interacts and grows. It shows us how much power has been bestowed upon each individual by having such a powerful medium readily available.

Member and Donor Engagement

The question about whether Twitter is here to stay is irrelevant. Conversational marketing is here to stay as long as the internet is open to real time discussion in public. While the platforms may change, Twitter-type communication provides an amazing amount of opportunity for the association professional. Twitter can help attract and retain members and donors, motivate groups of people, and identify supporters.

Attract Members and Donors

Twitter attracts an exponentially growing number of users. Those users include members and donors. When users provide links to resources that are valuable to their colleagues, members, donors, or the ephemeral "Twitterverse," they are adding value. Furthermore, when users share valuable links with their peers, they can potentially learn from it and grow professionally.

Motivate Groups of People

Examples abound when it comes to showing how influential social media can be for motivating people to support a cause or to raise money. On April 7, 2009, a cute video of an older couple playing piano was posted on the Sharing Mayo blog. Mayo's built in social media tools were used to share the video. The video was then featured on Good Morning America and resulted in more than 3.1 million views by June 8, 2009. A former CNN reporter named Veronica De La Cruz launched an effort to raise money for her brother's heart transplant in early May 2009. They raised more than $850,000 by May 28, 2009.

Identify Supporters

Clever associations can use Twitter to identify association supporters as well as to feed their industry's thought leaders with news that will spread their organization's message and add to their ability to serve their current membership. By monitoring and tracking keywords, associations can identify "influencers," people who *have the power to influence and persuade or have some kind of effect*. Influencers are the heart of word-of-mouth marketing. Influencers are used as a conduit to a target audience. They are listened to and looked up to, especially in times of a recession. A Twitter application called Klout attempts to measure influence for Twitter users by category.

Special Events

Association conferences like ASAE & the Center's Annual Meeting and major events like the E3 conference have shown what a great resource Twitter can be for quickly reporting news to a huge group of people. Faster and more immediate than a blog, Twitter has been embraced by the "new media" of the blogosphere and has slowly won acceptance among traditional media outlets.

At an association I used to work for, I was able to invite chapter leaders to an impromptu VIP party with the association's president because of Twitter. In the weeks approaching the annual meeting I gave all the chapter leaders my Twitter information (and guidance on how to use Twitter). After the more than 120 chapter leaders had broken from their leadership meeting for the day, I learned of a new invitation to all of them to meet with the organization's president. I sent out an alert via Twitter, and the turnout for the party that evening was successful, with members spilling out into the hallway. Those who were not connected to Twitter via their phone or internet had heard about it from those chapter leaders who had received the message. This simple but effective example of the power of technology as well as word of mouth made the association president a true believer in social media.

In 2008, Andy Steggles moderated an unofficial, unsanctioned session at ASAE & the Center's annual conference. Details of the event were deliberately kept secret as a way of trying to generate buzz via intrigue. Updates about the time and location were announced via twitter and Facebook the day before the event, and less than one hour before the event, the location had to be changed. The "Secret Session" attracted more than 200 attendees and was one of the most highly attended sessions of the conference. It wasn't even in the program.

Summary

Twitter can be a massive time drain, but it can also be an amazingly effective channel for mobilizing large groups of people and engaging members and donors. Twitter is ever evolving and so there will surely be new applications and functions within it that will streamline some of the processes outlined here. Ultimately, no matter what happens to the platform, the message is the same: Engagement is vital for associations. Might you hear about someone's breakfast in a 140-character tweet? Maybe. However, it is worth it if that person's next message is a link to an article transforming the way you do business.

CHAPTER 6

Evolving Educational Applications for Social Networking for Nonprofits

By Thomas C. Stewart, Ph.D.

"Once a new technology rolls over you," points out Stewart Brand, one of the founders of the Whole Earth Catalog, "if you're not part of the steamroller, you're part of the road." So how can you be part of the steamroller and not part of the road when it comes to social networking? It's not easy; it takes vision. The internet has evolved rapidly since the early 1990s, with some one-time successful business models, such as providing dial-up access, coming and going while new ones, such as mobile and social networking, coming into prominence.[1,12] One area that has been successful and continues to be is the delivery of educational programs through the internet.

Traditional associations and universities have been, in many cases, slow to adapt, and start-ups from the for-profit sector quickly filled the gap, with the University of Phoenix, Kaplan University, and Capella University being just a few of examples of for-profit universities offering programs online.[2,3] Although a little bit late to the game, nonprofits have started to play catch-up in a big way, leveraging their existing intellectual capital into a growing number of online programs, often cooperating with universities in the process.[6] For the consumer, the marketplace now offers a multitude of programs that can be completed without ever stepping onto a university campus or into a classroom. Online learning has led to a complete and profound shift in what the experience of getting educational credits is like for many types of students and association members.

Associations have made successful forays into the areas of continuing and professional education. The potential reach of online educational offerings is vast for these groups, as their very own membership bases are an excellent source of potential participants. Well-designed course offerings can build the reputation of the organization while providing a lucrative revenue stream through an already existing learning management system (LMS). With the added dimension of social networking, these types of offerings can become a cornerstone of developing and expanding the reach and influence of a nonprofit organization.

One key dynamic of the social web is how it has made us all teachers—and all students. Just as blogging has made us all citizen journalists, social media tools and resources have enabled us to share our knowledge and skills, learn from one another, and contribute and improve upon resources.

Institutional Knowledge

Often, associations find themselves relying on specific instructors to teach courses that the instructors have crafted. By turning these courses into online offerings while retaining the rights to the course, the association can reduce the risk of relying on a single subject matter expert and essentially institutionalize the knowledge by maintaining the updated course in an online environment.

Evolution of Online Course Offerings

Historically, the initial forays into online course offerings mirrored their immediate predecessors—the correspondence course. The correspondence course was truly asynchronous, non-live offering in which instructor and student worked at different times in different places. Often, courses were developed and students could sign up at any time and work at their own pace to complete the work. Materials were sent back and forth through the mail (thus the term mail-order degree), and the instructor and student knew relatively little about one another. Early online courses, using the best technology of the day, used static websites where students would receive assignments and send them to the instructor, in many cases still through the mail.

Traditional Educational Institutions

Developments in technology for traditional educational institutions have been revolutionary. Software companies have developed platforms, such as WebCT and Blackboard, that serve as online classrooms. Programs, such as Elluminate Live and Wimba, allow for synchronous learning, with instructors and students meeting at the same time in different places through online meetings that feature live chat and videoconferencing. Software by companies such as VirtualU, mirroring public web-based platforms such as Second Life, offer a new type of learning option featuring a true virtual space with avatar characters selected and designed by participants and online classrooms with virtual desks, chairs, and chalkboards. These new internet-based approaches offer a way of reaching the generation weaned on cell phones, Blackberries, text messaging, and constant connection in the way they are most used to: wired or, perhaps more accurately, wireless. While a course with a social networking component isn't meant to be better than a traditional classroom approach, it is superior to the earlier versions of correspondence courses. Furthermore, it does offer a valid option for those who would not be able to participate in a course with a traditional approach because of scheduling or location.

Augmenting the Learning Environment

How can the social web augment the learning environment? By itself, it is difficult. Taking the blended approach is a much surer way of having success. There are several key components. You can create a fusion of in-person meetings and an online component and tie it together with social web activities that support discussion groups and sharing of user-generated content. You can have online library repositories where selected peers can comment on, review, and rate their individual or group work. By combining existing workshops and learning modules, you can create a new way of delivering learning. No longer are your participants expected to turn up in a classroom or a conference room for a two-day workshop, remember (or forget) everything, and then leave. Now, the dialogue continues. The discussions that develop in the initial environment are extended with things such as regularly scheduled microexams, where participants compete against their peers to see who retains the most knowledge on the subject of the original workshop.

Ultimately, the social web is all about community. Fostering a small group of people from disparate backgrounds and interests into a permanent presence where they can leverage their peer-to-peer connections, creates a great resource. This is particularly true when the instructor or moderator is part of the group, and participants constantly bounce ideas and suggestions off of one another.

Pitfalls

What are some of the pitfalls of incorporating social networking? The biggest danger is going all-in without carefully examining the market. Take a close look at your current educational offerings and assess where you are. Establish a realistic set of goals and a budget that minimizes the risk. One of the easiest ways to avoid major risk is to pilot social networking as part of an existing training program. Adding a social networking component to a workshop that is part of an annual conference will help gauge interest while giving insights into the administrative support needed. If you have never provided online education, try dipping your toes in the water by providing a series of online webinars that can also be used to promote your in-person courses.

In January 2010, the American Evaluation Association (AEA) began a "Coffee Break Demonstration Series" of 20-minute webinars that highlighted tools, websites, and software of interest to its members. AEA Executive Director Susan Kistler, says, "We're using this program to meet many of our strategic goals while easing into offering webinar-based training. For each offering, we encourage use of association-branded social media to continue the conversation, provide links to related content in our community library, and in most cases, have the facilitator contribute to our blog. Having 400 registrants for our first offering suggests that our members are ready and willing to engage via this medium. It is our responsibility to meet that challenge."

Benefits

So what are the benefits of online course offerings, and how does social networking fit into the picture? One of the biggest benefits is flexibility. Effectively developed and designed online courses can continue to generate revenues long after the initial investment with relatively minimal updating and course coordination through your existing learning management system (LMS) framework. The courses and workshops can be offered at different times to best meet the demands of the market. And marketing itself can be done through existing outreach efforts, such as conferences and websites already run by nonprofit organizations and associations. Such courses can be synchronous or asynchronous, and they can either be stand-alone or offered as an extension of a special interest group developed at a conference or workshop. Facilitators can be drawn from among internal members who are known as subject matter experts, giving new reasons for members to be actively involved in the organization. Adding in a social networking piece to this approach adds a whole new dimension that promises to offer an enhanced sense of belonging to participants, further helping them identify with the brand of the organization offering such a course.

There are many ways to integrate a social network into the existing learning environment, most differ depending on the rest of the infrastructure. For example, if an association does not even have a website, let alone an association management system (AMS) or LMS, then a private platform is likely not a realistic possibility. Instead, other open/free platforms, such as NING, Facebook, Groupsites, LinkedIn, Wordpress, or perhaps even gotowebinar.com, could be used. Where possible, use public platforms primarily as outposts that push members back to your own website or central hub. Public platforms are not recommended because they lack any sort of integration with your main membership/donor database. Normally the organization would have, at the very least, an AMS and ideally an LMS.

To help understand the opportunities, consider the fictitious example of the Association of Widget Makers (AWM). The AWM is holding a two-day workshop during the summer in New York City. We'll assume that AWM has an AMS but not an LMS.

First AWM will need a social platform. The social platform will allow for community groups to be created, friends to be connected, and resources to be shared. Since the social platform is integrated into the AMS, the system creates a community dynamically by virtue of the event being in the AMS and the members being registered. The community will be created with a discussion group and library, and the registrants/attendees will be automatically registered with the community and subscribed to the discussion groups.

Shortly before the event, the instructor would send a welcome message to the class, inviting students to review the course documentation, study work, and any other complementary materials in the community's resource library. The instructor tells the class how many people are in the group and requests that registrants ensure their profiles (with photos) are up to date and, once they are, then asks everyone to "reply to all," introducing themselves. The instructor also offers a link to see the community home page where all attendees can see the rest of the participants.

Everyone then meets in person at the live conference in New York City already having some knowledge of who else is attending the course. As in a regular course, they tend to bond over the two days, but at the end of the in-person course, the instructor reminds the class about the final three exercises over the next three months, which are part of the course and are required to be completed to receive the continuing education credits.

Immediately after the course ends, the instructor posts the PowerPoint presentations for the course with a thank-you note for everyone's participation, together with a link to the first online exercise. The interesting thing about this exercise is that the first group exercise is to answer four specific questions about the course topic using a wiki. In other words, the group will collaboratively answer the questions, with each person allowed to modify and update the previous person's response. Combine the collaborative nature of a wiki with the associated discussion group and resource library, and the traditional online course becomes much more dynamic and immersive.

This is just one example of how to integrate a social platform into an AMS. Obviously, the scenario would change depending on the elements you have in place. If you already have an LMS, the first step would be to approach your provider and ask if any social networking components or partners are embedded in the software and if a set of best practices is available. The gains are many-fold if the offerings are designed properly and acknowledge potential pitfalls. There are certainly major differences between traditional instructional approaches and online approaches, differences that can be mitigated by using basic social network integration or more immersive 3D virtual environments as extensions of a traditional course or workshop.[8] By adding social networking, course designers are adding a new dimension that enhances the participant's educational and networking experiences through immersive technologies. Furthermore, associations and other educational providers that take full advantage of the potential methodologies of social networking enhance their educational products as well as their brands. Offering a workshop that extends beyond the usual window of a few days that most conferences last and turns into something far more substantial and rewarding for the participants will naturally reflect positively on the organization.

Pitfalls

Security Issues

Those investigating adding social networking to existing educational programs need to ensure that they have proper security. Identity theft is a broad concern that has gained increased attention over the years.[4,5,11] Obviously, it would be devastating for any organization—nonprofit or otherwise—to receive the negative publicity of being held responsible for releasing personal information into the hands of cyber-criminals. When adding a social networking component, keep in mind that there is usually no need to collect an abundance of personal data.

Privacy Risks and Culture

A bigger concern is allowing participants to control who has access to them even within their group.[7] For example, it is possible to create a follow-up group using an existing platform such as Facebook. The downside is that approach may unintentionally lead to too much sharing. Participants who already use Facebook as a personal website may feel uncomfortable letting professional associates see too much of their private side—photos with family members and friends, personal musings, and the like. Using a platform such as Second Life, in which participants create their own avatars, can also cause a potentially uncomfortable blurring between personal and professional elements of participants' lives. Either they do not feel comfortable enough to sign up at all, or they unintentionally end up giving out or receiving too much personal information that is unrelated to the course or workshop. Part of making it successful, then, is to allow the social networking to take place in an environment where participants feel comfortable about who else has information about them and what that information is.

Other Challenges

With any new technology or approach, there are some distinct challenges, and they need to be addressed carefully before forging ahead. One of the biggest challenges for nonprofits trying to incorporate social media is that there are three pieces to the puzzle: the association management system (AMS) or its equivalent, the learning management system (LMS), and the social platform itself. How do you tie them together? Figuring that out—and getting it right—is one of the keys to success. With the onset of open web services, this is becoming easier to do as long as your AMS and LMS support open architecture—they have web services available to be consumed by third party products. This can be addressed by checking with your internal IT staff or hiring a qualified IT consultant to give you assurance about existing capabilities. If your systems do support open architecture, then you can start right away. If not, you will need to decide whether to make changes to your system so that it will incorporate open architecture, or you may want to invest in custom programming to build the necessary web services to allow for the integration. The open architecture approach is recommended because it allows more flexibility, and since open is the direction of the future, you will be better positioned for such developments.

Small organizations with a non-integrated environment may take a more hands-on and time-consuming alternative, manually comparing internal lists to the participant lists in a public platform to ensure the right people are in the environment you have created. Alternatively, you could leave the group wide open and simply give up control of it. Doing so may dilute the value of the member benefit, but if it is a choice of this or nothing, it might be a viable option.

Other challenges exist. Moderators or instructors who are teaching online should familiarize themselves with adaptive pedagogical strategies associated with teaching online.[14,16] Because this environment is likely to be as new for your workshop moderators as it is for the participants, a train-the-trainer session will be important. Moderators must know the programs well enough themselves to be able to provide detailed instructions to participants as well as to anticipate questions about how things work. Nothing will derail the social networking element more quickly than a design that is too complex for the casual, infrequent user to navigate. After all, if participants in a workshop are asked to revisit the social networking component three weeks after the initial meeting, you want to have a user interface that is easy to use and can be navigated intuitively.

A Window on the Future

Dan enters the wood-paneled conference room, taking a seat in a cushioned chair on the left. A bank of windows on the right looks out on a tree-filled courtyard with a fountain. Dan looks to the front of the room, where the moderator stands at the podium waiting to start. Turning to his right, Dan sees some of the other participants, men and women from a variety of backgrounds. He knows most of them from a previous workshop—some quite well. They wave to him, and he waves back as he waits for the room to fill. Most of them wear standard business attire, but there are a couple of notable exceptions: a beefy man wearing a Hawaiian shirt and shorts and a woman wearing a Reebok track suit. The moderator is new, so Dan decides to find out more about her background. He clicks on her face and a pop-up window opens above her head, displaying an extract of her professional social profile from the association member directory; it gives her name, title, contact information, and a link to her full profile. As he looks at this, he hears a beep; one of the other participants he knows is sending him a chat message. He responds by clicking on her face. Just then, the moderator begins speaking. Dan clicks on the podium to access her notes.

What is happening here? Welcome to the virtual world—a 3D virtual classroom where all participants can interact with their environment from literally any connected place in the world.

The start of the above situation would describe any standard conference or workshop, down to setting, décor, and dress—well, at least most of the dress. And yet this is not the real world; it's a virtual world created to simulate the real one, down to the smallest details. The room has been designed to look like the original room where these participants met more than a month earlier. By clicking on any of the other participants, Dan can find out whatever information they have decided to share. Those he knows can allow more access, giving out personal e-mails and Facebook access; whereas, others may post just their professional information. Dan can do the same, having control over who gets access to what. He has chosen and designed his own avatar to represent himself and his business. He reveals that his full name is Daniel, but most of his old friends still call him Danny. When looking around the room, he controls who has access to all of this information. Dan knows Amy, who put her avatar in a tracksuit, as a Reebok employee and a friend. When she puts her mouse over his avatar, she has access to all of his profile. The access level is determined by the permissions Dan has set in the association's member directory privacy preferences. Since Amy is a "trusted" connection, she can see all his professional profile. Max, represented by the avatar with the Hawaiian shirt, owns a travel company. He currently does not have access to Dan's profile; he will need to initiate a "friend" request that is driven through the social platform (member directory).

Participants can have fun with their avatars. In Dan's case, he's not quite as fit as his avatar, which he thinks is funny. And his hair is a little bit grayer around the edges and thinner on top. In this space, regardless of the details, the avatar becomes the virtual representation of the participant. Participants control the design of the avatar and what information they share and with whom. Technology developed by VirtualU and others for business conferencing can be easily adapted for educational applications that can serve as a social networking follow-up to a traditional course or seminar. Properly introduced, the creation of profiles and avatars can be an enjoyable exercise for participants that will help them bond. To make social networking follow-up successful, networking definitely should be included as part of a scheduled online workshop. Expecting participants to do it later in their own time often means it never gets done.

Case Study: 3D Virtual World Annual Conference[17]

Six months after its annual conference in 2008, the Risk & Insurance Management Society, Inc. (RIMS) hosted a two-day virtual conference, RiskLive!, complete with exhibitors, 14 educational sessions, and networking lounges. The goal was to extend the one-week annual conference experience that RIMS offers. Nonmembers were charged a $50 registration fee, while RIMS members could register for no cost.

RIMS employed Digitell to build a virtual world that could accommodate more attendees than many other virtual applications, which can crash if too many users are in the simulation at one time.

To market the conference, Digitell made two videos for RIMS to send via email, one targeted to exhibitors and one to attendees, showing avatars walking in the world and watching sessions. (View one video at http://bit.ly/risklive.) RIMS also tested various email marketing styles to attract more registrants. Staff members outside the marketing department were asked to write emails that would compel them to act. The styles were different. In one instance, the plain text email generated twice the response rate of the HTML email.

Over two days, RiskLive! gathered more than 500 attendees and 20 exhibitor booths customized with streaming video, company backgrounds, and quick links to online services. Because it was such a new technology, many exhibitors wanted to wait to see how it went, but since then, more exhibitors have expressed interest in a future offering.

Most participants said the greatest value was education, not necessarily networking. One session alone had 120 people. After the event, RIMS surveyed its members and asked if it were a mistake to try this new approach. The answer was overwhelmingly no. Members were pleased that RIMS was trying new things. It was a vote of confidence from members.

Getting Started

Blended Offerings

Numerous models exist for applying a social network element to your educational offerings. The blended model, combining an existing onsite course or workshop with a follow-up piece using social networking and/or a 3D virtual space, offers a chance to get into social networking with the safety net of the face-to-face modality with which you are already familiar. Some key questions should be addressed first:

- Do we have the IT support, including hardware and software, to do this? What is the overhead? How will we recoup costs, or do we need to?
- How will we train staff facilitators to use this? How will we support member questions?
- How often will we interact with clients?
- How much client training will we build into our existing workshop (how to navigate the virtual space, create an avatar, and other basics)?
- How will we manage security?

Without leveraging a Software as a Service (SaaS) offering or owning the hardware and software, it's unlikely you will be able to run this type of environment successfully. There's no point in spending time and effort developing a social networking component on the front end only to find that there's no one to manage it once it is up and running. Confused participants will quickly become nonparticipants, and that will reflect poorly on your organization and your educational offerings. A help line (often but not always managed by the platform provider) as well as a Frequently Asked Questions (FAQs) page should be in place before you start.

The workshop/course facilitators must be fluent in the technology as well. One of the best ways to avoid a lot of back-end confusion among participants is to have facilitators who are able to clearly and effectively teach using the platform. If the participants leave the conference or workshop with a solid understanding of how to navigate the platform, whether it is Blackboard, Elluminate Live, VirtualU, or something else, you will spend much less follow-up time—and money—on helping participants and the participants themselves will be much more satisfied.

Security is always a concern because it is one area you cannot afford to get wrong. One solution is not to collect more information than you need. If you don't have it, you don't need to protect it. Do you really need Social Security numbers or home phone numbers? Build in security protocols on the front-end, and make sure staff members are well aware of them. Ensure that the security protocols that are part of your AMS are also part of your LMS.

Online-Only Offerings

While the blended model may be the recommended one for getting started, going all-in with a 100 percent online offering with a social networking element can be successful, too. Before doing that, ask these questions in addition to those posed for blended models:

- Who will be responsible for maintaining the virtual space?
- Will it be synchronous or asynchronous? If synchronous, how will the schedule be determined?
- How will we market the course/workshop?

If it is a 100 percent online offering, it is important that you have a dedicated set of personnel, including a point person to manage the online offering. For a single course, that could be one person. For a more complex offering, you may need a team of people with specific responsibilities. A key consideration is whether you offer synchronous sessions with live online meetings using VirtualU, Elluminate Live, or another platform or whether you use an asynchronous environment where participants can view prepared materials at their convenience. The live meetings have major advantages in terms of bonding and identity. They create a more complete experience. However, synchronous meetings are much more labor-intensive for the facilitator and the participants. The facilitator must dedicate time for running the sessions. Also, you need to pick times when participants will be able to join. When all of your participants are from a similar geographic region, this is not as much of a challenge. But when they are spread over the country or even the world, be prepared to address time zone issues with synchronous courses. Sessions can be recorded with nearly all software platforms, meaning even asynchronous offerings can provide an enriched multimedia experience.

Finally, there is the issue of marketing. Blended courses, because they are extensions of traditional face-to-face workshops or meetings, are an extension and enrichment of something already being done. The marketing, therefore, needs to be built into what you have. For completely online courses, you have to reach participants in new ways. Existing email and mailing lists are certainly a start. To grab someone's attention enough to get a registrant, though, the information should include specific examples of what participants will get for their investment. For virtual environments, try using video teasers that reveal the extent of online virtual interaction. Ensure you build and budget your marketing plan in your initial planning. After all, it would be futile to pour money into course development only to find few, if any, participants have registered. For larger programs, it might be worthwhile to bring in a marketing consultant who specializes in online offerings.

Be the Steamroller...or Become a Snail Kite?

Ever hear of the snail kite? This small, falcon-like bird feeds exclusively on the apple snail. Both are found only in the Everglades, which have been altered dramatically by the massive influx of people into Florida in the last few decades. Since its habitat has changed so quickly, the apple snail is unable to adapt and is dramatically decreasing in numbers and, therefore, the snail kite has less prey. Because these creatures are so specialized and unable to adapt, they are threatened with extinction. Both are hanging on, but they are hobbled by their inability to change with their environment and have essentially lost control of their own destinies.[10] Don't let this happen to your organization in regard to your educational offerings and the ability to integrate social networking as a key component. Nobody wants to be just hanging on. Failure to adapt to the possibilities can diminish your organization's long-term growth potential.

With connectivity so entrenched in our society and with the advent of social networking as a way of using the technology, combined with the evolution of online educational technology, it is time to get on board or be rolled over. A September 2008 blog on the American Society of Association Executives (ASAE) website[9] posed the question, "Are associa-tions going extinct?" Those that do not adapt certainly face that possibility just as surely as do the snail kite and the apple snail. One of the areas cited as changing the game is the new dynamics of social networking. Associations and nonprofits that do not take advantage of the new technologies risk being marginalized by them. The good news is that these new technologies offer a chance to expand the reach of nonprofits and associations that incorporate them.

Two decades ago, few companies had any presence on the internet, and now a web presence is considered de rigueur. Ten years ago, conferences and workshops were the main avenues for associations and nonprofits to offer bonding and identity-creating experiences for their members. The explosion in social networking capabilities and the possibilities of 3D virtual-learning environments offer a new way to engage people in a way that may significantly increase the importance of your organization to your members. People are already using social networking to connect with friends and family outside a work environment; Facebook alone has topped the 350 million user mark.[13] Today, hours spent on the internet far exceed those spent watching television.[15] You can make your organization part of those hours, part of that world. The new technology is there. It can be easily integrated into existing offerings, or it can allow you to expand in ways heretofore unimaginable. Don't limit yourself like the snail kite. Learn the new technology and take advantage of it. Be the steamroller, and let someone else be the road.

References

1. Banks, A. *On the Way to the Web: The Secret History of the Internet and its Founders.* Berkeley, CA: Apress. 2008.
2. Blumenstyk, G. For-profit education: Online courses fuel growth. *The Chronicle of Higher Education,* 51 (18), Jan 2005. A11.
3. Bradley, G. For-profit online education receives a boon. *Academe,* 92 (3), May/June, 2006.
4. Britt, P. Identity thieves hit a new low. *Information Today,* 26 (2), Feb 2007. 1, 43-44.
5. Caeton, D. A. The cultural phenomenon of identity theft and the domestication of the World Wide Web. *Bulletin of Science, Technology, & Society,* 27 (1), Feb 2007. 11-23.
6. Carnevale, D. Liberal-arts colleges create joint effort for online courses. *The Chronicle of Higher Education,* 52 (25), Feb 24, 2006. A33.
7. Couros, A. Safety and social networking. *Technology & Learning,* 28 (7), Feb, 2008. 20-22.
8. Jones, J. G., Morales, C., & Knezek, G. A. *Educational Media International,* 42 (3), 2005. 219-236.

9. Latest from the blogs: Are associations going extinct? ASAECenter.org., Sept 2008.

10. Licona, P. Personal interview. Oct 5, 2009.

11. Marshall, A. M., & Tompsett, B. C. Identity theft in an online world. *Computer Law & Security Report*, 21 (2), March, 2005. 128-137.

12. Okin, J.A. *The Internet Revolution: The Not-for-Dummies Guide to the History, Technology, and Use of the Internet.* Winter Harbor, ME: Ironbound Press. 2005.

13. Oreskovic, A. Facebook makes money, tops 300 million users. CalgaryHerald.com. Sept 15, 2009.

14. Palloff, R. M., & Pratt, K. *Building Online Learning Communities: Effective Strategies for the Virtual Classroom.* San Francisco: Jossey-Bass. 2008.

15. Sachoff, M. Internet outpacing TV for time spent. WebProNews.com. Feb 19, 2008.

16. Shank, P. *The Online Learning Idea Book: 95 Proven Ways to Enhance Technology-Based and Blended Learning.* San Francisco: Pfeiffer. 2008.

17. Steggles, A. Personal interview. May 1, 2009.

CHAPTER 7

Legal Risk and Liabilities on the Social Web

By Barbara F. Dunn, Nathan J. Breen, and Joshua W. Peterson from Howe & Hutton, Ltd.

Web 2.0—the next generation of the internet—is here. Electronic media applications such as online bulletin boards, listservers, blogs, and social networking sites have become essential tools for associations for sharing information with their members and for members to share information with each other—information relevant to their own industries. The developments, however, do not come without risk, and anyone who participates in online media—including associations and nonprofits that choose to operate their own listservers, blogs, and bulletin boards—should be aware of the legal issues and liabilities that accompany these outlets. This chapter focuses on United States law but may be used to generate ideas about what needs to be considered from an international perspective.

The most important consideration for associations that create and monitor their own Web 2.0 applications is to create a user agreement and to rigidly enforce its terms. While monitoring their own applications, associations should also pay particular attention to intellectual property rights and monitor their sites for any potentially defamatory content. As a final defense, associations should check their general liability insurance policies to ensure that they have coverage for claims arising from their internet-based activities.

The other situation to which associations must pay careful attention is when their members contribute to third-party applications, such as Facebook, LinkedIn, and Twitter, in connection with their association memberships. Although members generally have First Amendment rights in what they communicate on websites unaffiliated with the association, such speech has the potential to generate liability for the association. Associations cannot exert control over their members' speech, but they can implement social media policies to detach themselves from a liability perspective. This chapter offers insight into ways that an association can exert control over its members' speech from afar so that it will have a better chance of avoiding liability arising from members' speech.

Applications and Websites Controlled by Associations

Communications Decency Act

Associations that choose to implement and monitor listservers or online bulletin boards on their own websites should be familiar with the requirements of the Communications Decency Act (47 U.S.C. § 230) (CDA) and the policies behind it. In a general sense, the CDA was passed to promote an online marketplace of ideas where material can be exchanged freely, but it is also designed to encourage internet service providers to monitor their forums to decrease offensive material. By encouraging this free exchange of ideas, Congress wanted to minimize the tort liability of internet service providers whose main purpose is to disseminate information, not create it.

By way of background, a few early court decisions, the most notable of which was *Stratton Oakmont, Inc. v. Prodigy Services Co.,* 1995 WL 323710 (N.Y. Sup. Ct. 1995), held that the provider of an online forum, such as a bulletin board or listserver, could be held liable as a publisher of the material that appears within the forum where the host exercised editorial control over its content. The *Stratton Oakmont* court held that an Internet Service Provider (ISP) (companies such as AOL, Prodigy, and Compuserve that provide individuals and other companies access to the internet and other related services such as website building and virtual hosting) that holds itself out to the public and its subscribers as controlling the content of its computer bulletin boards and uses an automatic screening program and/or employees to delete notes on its bulletin board that were offensive or in "bad taste" will be treated as a "publisher." As such, they will be responsible for content posted on its computer bulletin boards. These cases had the unfortunate effect of dissuading ISPs to monitor their own bulletin boards and listservers for objectionable content.

In response to *Stratton Oakmont,* Congress enacted the CDA, which overruled *Stratton Oakmont* and provides that "[n]o provider or user of an interactive computer service shall be treated as the publisher or speaker of any information provided by another information content provider." As long as the content was written by a third party rather than the ISP itself, the ISP is immune from liability. Note that, based on the definition of an ISP in the CDA, associations that operate interactive computer services would qualify as ISPs.

The CDA does not grant full immunity to ISPs, however. It does not cover allegations involving the violation of a criminal statute, the infringement of intellectual property, and a website's inducement or encouragement of illegal activity. Furthermore, the CDA applies only to claims under United States law. Associations with international members and associations that appeal to international audiences should be aware that ISPs are not awarded similar protections abroad. Courts in other countries will hold ISPs liable for speech posted by third parties that violates the laws of the particular country, particularly those that can be equated to our First Amendment freedom of speech. See *Yahoo!, Inc. v. La Ligue Contre Le Racisme Et L'Antisemitisme,* 433 F.3d 1199 (9th Cir. 2006).

To stay within the bounds of the CDA, associations providing Web 2.0 applications should stay neutral in terms of monitoring content and consider prescreening content only to eliminate defamatory or irrelevant material.

Create and Enforce Terms of a User Agreement

To implement an effective approach toward monitoring a listserver or bulletin board, an association should first formulate a policy statement concerning the purpose of the bulletin board or listserver and communicate the policy statement to its members and staff. Also, since listservers or bulletin boards are the association's proprietary forum, the association is free to put whatever restrictions on its use it sees fit. Therefore, associations should develop a comprehensive user agreement that all bulletin board or listserver participants agree to before accessing or being permitted continued access to the forum. It should then consistently follow and enforce its own policy. For specific items to include in the terms of use/user agreement, the association should consult its attorney. Below are some essential provisions that every terms of use/user agreement should contain.

- Inform users that the listserver or blog functions as a private forum administered by the association and may be used only with the association's permission in accordance with the user agreement. Since the association controls access to the forum, it can make users—whether they are members or nonmembers—subject to the terms of the user agreement.
- Specify terms of eligibility for use of the forum.
- Specify the focus of the forum and identify what types of content are unacceptable and require the user to agree not to use the forum for improper or illegal purposes. The association can specify that only content which adds to the body of knowledge regarding the association and its field(s) of interest are permitted.
- Inform the user about the association's monitoring practice.
- Representations and warranties: Require users to represent that all statements and information they submit are accurate.
- Require the user to indemnify, defend, and hold the association harmless for any claims brought as a result of user's use of the forum.
- Specify any disciplinary measures that may be taken as a result of any improper use of the forum. If the user violates the user agreement, the association may terminate the user's right to participate and reserves the right to terminate the user's membership. (You must enforce measures consistently and uniformly.)
- Identify governing law and require the user to consent to a certain jurisdiction in the event that the user agreement is breached.

Finally, consider posting the link or icon for the terms of use agreement in the upper left-hand quadrant of the homepage. In any dispute concerning the actual acceptance of the terms, a court is likely to take judicial notice that internet pages open and are read from the upper left-hand quadrant. Therefore, a potential plaintiff will have to overcome the presumption that he or she did not see the link or the icon. (Bick, Jonathan and Karen Berger, "Enforceable Browse-Wrap Contracts." *Internet Law & Strategy*, Volume 7, Number 10, October 2009, pg. 5).

Note that it is important for the association to have users properly "execute" the user agreement. This is typically accomplished by displaying the user agreement in a dialog box and having the user click to indicate acceptance of the agreement. These types of "click wrap" agreements are enforceable. The association can also provide a link on the system so that the user can return to view the agreement at a later date. As noted below, it is critical for the association to maintain proper records as to date and time of acceptance of the user agreement.

Intellectual Property Considerations

Comply with Copyright Laws

The Online Copyright Infringement Liability Limitation Act (OCILLA), (17 U.S.C. § 512) was passed as part of the 1998 Digital Millennium Copyright Act and is intended as a shield for internet service providers from monetary damages as a result of copyright infringement by users. An ISP's liabilities will be limited as long as it first adopts and reasonably implements a policy of addressing infringement and terminating accounts of users who are found to be repeat infringers. ISPs must also accommodate and not interfere with "standard technical measures" used by copyright owners to identify infringement. Limited liability exists as long as the ISP is engaging in one of the following four categories of conduct: (i) transitory communications, (ii) system caching, (iii) storage of information on systems or networks at the direction of users, and (iv) information location tools. OCILLA also includes special rules concerning the application of these limitations to nonprofit educational institutions.

A copyright is a property right in an original work of authorship such as an article, book, picture, music, or software. The owner of the copyright has the following bundle of exclusive rights that begin the moment the work is created:

- The right to copy the work;

- The right to control others' use of the work in derivative fashions (e.g., create a workbook based on a textbook or translate a work into another language) and to control what is done with the copyrighted work;
- The right to publicly distribute the work;
- The right to publicly display the work; and
- The right to publicly perform the copyright work.

Note that the last three ownership rights relate to use of the work "publicly" which is defined as any use outside the scope of family and friends. In other words, any association meeting or trade show would be considered "public" under federal copyright law even though the public is not invited.

Federal registration of a copyright is recommended but not necessary unless the owner sues for federal copyright infringement. The person who created the work owns the work unless the work was created by an independent contractor or volunteer. In such circumstances, a written agreement must specify that the association owns the work. A work created by an employee within the scope of his or her employment is owned by the employer.

Copyright owners can display the © symbol from the moment the work is created; no federal registration of the work is needed to display the symbol. A sample copyright notice may read:

> ©Copyright [year(s) of first publication]. [Name of Association], [City, State, and Country of Office(s)] [All rights reserved. No right of reproduction without the prior written consent of [Name of Association]]. (Or Reproduction permitted with credit to [Name of Association].)

Note that an association cannot use another copyright owner's work without permission. Use without such permission constitutes copyright infringement. Fair use is a defense to copyright infringement but should not be heavily relied on because copyright owners may overcome fair use defense if the particular use diminishes the market for the copyrighted work.

Comply with Trademark Laws

Trademarks generally consist of words or symbols that identify a source and distinguish the goods or services in connection with the context in which they are used from the goods or services of others. Trademarks are used in connection with goods; service marks are used in connection with services. Most association marks are service marks.

Federal registration is recommended but not necessary. Owners establish "common law" rights from the moment the mark is used. However, federal registration affords more protection and a basic presumption of ownership rights in the mark. To legally use the ® symbol, the mark must be federally registered. Associations may use TM (trademarks) and SM (service marks) for marks not yet registered or while registration is pending.

Use of another's trademark without permission in a manner which is likely to cause confusion constitutes trademark infringement, which can result in liability for damages.

Monitor for Defamation

Defamation is defined as the making and publishing of false statements about a person that damage his or her reputation. The person making the statement must have known or should have known that the statement was false. Generally, a corporate entity may be defamed by remarks about its financial condition, honesty, integrity, and so on. Truth is the best defense to a claim of defamation. Therefore, associations and their members must always make sure they are making accurate statements when communicating facts.

Statements of opinion may also give rise to a claim of defamation. A potential defendant will have a valid claim of defamation only if the statement appears to be based on specific facts and an express allegation of those facts would be defamatory. For example, the statement, "I do not think Association Y's promotion of the widget industry has been ethical" implies personal knowledge of dishonest conduct by Association Y and may be actionable. Unlike a basic statement of fact, whether a statement of opinion such as this example is in fact actionable depends on the circumstances surrounding the publication and the nature of the words used. The speaker may supply facts to elaborate on his or her statement of opinion, thereby backing it up with truthful facts.

Associations and their members must be extra cautious that they do not make defamatory statements on Web 2.0 applications. Whereas newspapers and magazines normally have local readership or can be cost prohibitive for many people to read and industry-specific publications usually are not widely disseminated, the internet is extremely accessible and can reach billions of people. Therefore, damages can increase exponentially when defamation occurs on the web because of the widespread dissemination and easy access. Put simply, the more people that have read the defamatory statement, the greater the damage done to the victim's reputation.

Aside from the defense of truthfulness, some states have retraction laws that allow the publication to retract the defamatory statement. However, associations should not rely on this potential remedy because the statute may not be updated to account for internet technology. For example, the statute may specifically restrict the use of retraction to instances when the defamation occurs in a newspaper, magazine, or periodical.

Though the Communications Decency Act will offer liability protection as described above, associations that operate Web 2.0 applications run the risk of claims from those alleged to have been defamed who argue the association should be held liable for helping to disseminate the defamatory communication. To combat the potential for financial liability for such statements, associations should ensure that all users have already agreed to indemnify the association in the user agreement.

Finally, depending on the context and content of the statement, a defamatory remark may also give rise to a claim for intentional interference with economic advantage. Associations should therefore be wary about members' remarks concerning their competitors.

Associations should not only monitor their own Web 2.0 applications for potential defamatory statements made by their own members but also continually remind their members to tune into what their competitors and other associations in similar industries are saying about them. The information detailed above should encourage associations to be vigilant about what other associations' websites are claiming about them and to deal with defamation issues as they arise.

Final Word—Liability Insurance

Associations should check their general liability insurance policies to ensure that they have coverage for claims arising from their internet-based activities. This would include a review of the association's general liability, directors and officers, and publisher liability insurance policies.

Association and Member Participation on Third-Party Websites

Often members of associations will branch out and exchange ideas through various social media not controlled by the association. Twitter, Facebook, LinkedIn, blogs, wikis, and other electronic bulletin boards have become effective ways to broadcast one's thoughts. While associations cannot control what their members do or say in non-association forums, associations can advise their members to be careful when publishing statements pertaining to current events and issues relevant to the industry and to keep an eye on what other members and nonmembers are saying about the association on social media. Associations should advise their members to:

- Follow terms of use, privacy policy, and content policy. The association should advise members to write and submit content under their own names and not "on behalf of the association" unless the association has given them prior approval to speak on its behalf.
- Comply with copyright laws. Materials produced by others should not be cited or referenced without their approval.
- Comply with trademark laws.
- Exercise caution when publishing statements pertaining to current events and issues relevant to the industry.
- Keep an eye on what other members and nonmembers are saying about the association.
- Exercise caution in that extensive participation in third party social media websites may cause damage to themselves and to the association as a whole.

Create Social Media Policy and Follow It

To ensure members understand the association's position on use of social media by its members, the association should develop a policy statement regarding social media and, most importantly, follow it uniformly and consistently. The policy statement can first state that the association encourages its members to participate in public discussions through social networking but, at the same time, the association expects that its members will make statements that are in the best interests of the association and will not engage in any inappropriate statements or statements that would be detrimental to the association as a whole. It is also important to inform members that the association retains the right, under its bylaws and policies, to take disciplinary actions against any member it determines is acting contrary to the association's interests. It is then up to the association to make the determination whether any statement is contrary to the association's interests. In that regard, the association may want to further elaborate that the expression of opinions is acceptable, but such opinions must be communicated in a professional manner.

Associations may also choose to require prior approval for members' establishment of a "group" on any social networking site. In other words, any group that wants to carry the organization's name or logo must ask for permission from the association to do so and agree to ensure that participants in the group comply with the association's social media policy. This is particularly difficult for creators of groups to enforce, since they cannot control the user agreement of a group created on LinkedIn, for example. This is another reason why it is safer for an association to host its own network or forums.

First Amendment Issues Related to Participation on Third-Party Websites

Since members' participation on third-party websites is speech in the electronic form, the First Amendment still applies. More specifically, the issues within the First Amendment that would govern participation on third-party websites are whether the member qualifies as a journalist—therefore receiving the same First Amendment freedoms granted to mainstream journalists—and defamation.

Blogger First Amendment Rights as Journalist?

Just because a person contributes to a blog does not make that person a journalist or afford that person the First Amendment protections given to journalists. The Monmouth County New Jersey Superior Court ruled on June 30, 2009, that a blogger does not necessarily qualify as a journalist for purposes of protecting the bloggers' sources. Journalists are given general protection from being required to reveal their sources. In this case, a blogger was sued by the software company Too Much Media for the blogger's criticism of the company on the blog Oprano, a website that proclaims itself the "Wall Street Journal of Porn." The court ruled that Too Much Media could ask the blogger for the identity of the sources for the comments she made on the blog. The court noted that courts "are now being faced with the task of evaluating a virtually limitless number of people who claim to be 'reporting' on issues, but who are, many times, doing little more than shouting from a digital soap box."

Associations and their members should be mindful of any complaints posted by nonmembers about them on blogs. They may have the right to challenge the blogger's message and require the blogger to reveal his or her sources if the blogger is not a bona fide journalist.

Defamation

The same concepts discussed above regarding defamation in the context of publication on an application controlled by an association apply to material submitted to third-party applications such as Facebook and Twitter. Associations should warn their members about the dangers of posting defamatory content on such websites, and they should advise their members to be vigilant about potential defamatory content that might be submitted concerning the association on third-party websites as well.

Internet Privacy

Privacy issues affect the members who post materials on third-party applications as well as those people or entities about which the communication was made. A recent case describes internet users' expectations of privacy while participating in online communication. Associations and their members should take a proactive approach and not simply hope for a court to decide in their favor if sued.

Based on the relative ease of transmitting data via the internet and the internet protocol requirement that content and data are duplicated by third parties along the way, one can argue that there is no reasonable expectation of privacy in internet communications. Recently, courts have attempted to grant the right to privacy with respect to internet communications on the grounds that it may be reasonably expected. Essentially, the common thread was that if it could be reasonably inferred based on the communication itself that the parties intended their communication to be private, the more likely it will be that a court would rule it as such.

Expectations of Communicating Parties

United States v. Maxwell, 45 M.J. 406, (C.A.A.F.1996) is an excellent case for purposes of explaining the court's traditional viewpoint on internet users' expectations of privacy. To start with, the court establishes that a person may challenge the validity of a government search by asserting a subjective expectation of privacy that is objectively reasonable under the circumstances. The *Maxwell* case involved a colonel in the U.S. Air Force who was accused of using his personal computer to send obscenity and child pornography to a fellow service member via AOL. AOL provides a certain level of privacy for its customers in that email messages are privately stored for retrieval on AOL's centralized and privately owned computer bank. At the time, its policy was not to read or disclose subscribers' email to anyone except authorized users, thus offering its own contractual privacy protection in addition to any federal statutory protections. Furthermore, it was AOL's policy not to disclose the communication to third parties absent a court order. Therefore, AOL users who send messages to other AOL subscribers have a contractual guarantee of privacy absent a court order.

In a general sense, therefore, users of personal computers start with a legitimate, objectively reasonable expectation of privacy in their own personal computers. See *United States v. Lifshitz*, 369 F.3d 173, 190 (2nd Cir. 2004) ("Individuals generally possess a reasonable expectation of privacy in their home computers."); see also *United States v. Buckner*, 473F.3d 551, 554 n. 2 (4th Cir. 2007) (recognizing a reasonable expectation of privacy in password-protected computer files); see also *Trulock v. Freeh*, 275 F.3d 391, 403 (4th Cir. 2001).

There are limitations to the expectation of privacy, however, under different, more subjective situations. The more open the method of transmissions, such as the "chat room," the less privacy one can reasonably expect. The internet has a less secure email system, in which messages must pass through a series of computers in order to reach the intended recipient. See *American Civil Liberties Union, et al. v. Reno,* 929 F.Supp. 824, 830-44 (E.D.Pa. 1996). Email messages sent to the public at large in a "chat room" or email that is "forwarded" from correspondent to correspondent loses any semblance of privacy. Once these transmissions are sent out to more and more subscribers, the subsequent expectation of privacy incrementally diminishes. Even in cases such as *Maxwell* where a user has a contractual expectation of privacy, there is no guarantee that the policy will be strictly followed and that the message will not be intercepted, copied, and redistributed against the user's wishes.

Members should keep this in mind when submitting content to Web 2.0 applications. Since a lawsuit to redress a potential invasion of privacy will obviously be costly and potentially embarrassing to the victim, it is advisable to abstain from posting any information that the user would not want redistributed.

Monitoring Policy

United States v. Heckenkamp, 482 F.3d 1142 (9th Cir. 2007) is a case that develops the expectation of privacy analysis in the *Maxwell* case a step further. The case involved a computer system administrator for Qualcomm Corporation who discovered that a graduate student at the University of Wisconsin had hacked into the Qualcomm's computer network while the student's computer was hooked up to the university's network. The student had hacked into the university's network system as well. The main issue before the Ninth Circuit Court was whether the student's objectively reasonable expectation of privacy in his computer was eliminated when he attached it to the university network. The Court concluded that based on the facts of the case that the act of attaching his computer to the network did not extinguish his legitimate, objectively reasonable privacy expectations.

A person's reasonable expectation of privacy may be diminished in "transmissions over the internet or emails that have already arrived at the recipient." See *United States v. Lifshitz,* 369 F.3d 173, 190 (2nd Cir. 2004).

However, the mere act of accessing a network does not in itself extinguish privacy expectations, nor does the fact that others may have occasional access to the computer. See *Leventhal v. Knapek*, 266 F.3d 64, 74 (2nd Cir. 2001). Moreover, privacy expectations may be reduced if the user is advised that information transmitted through the network is not confidential and that the system administrators may monitor communications transmitted by the user. See *United States v. Angevine*, 281 F.3d 1130, 1134 (10th Cir. 2002) *United States v. Simons*, 206 F.3d 392, 398 (4th Cir. 2000).

In *Heckenkamp*, there was no announced monitoring policy on the network, in the affirmative sense. Instead, the university's policy provided that "in general, all computer and electronic files should be free from access by any but the authorized users of those files. Exceptions to this basic principle shall be kept to a minimum and made only where essential to…protect the integrity of the University and the rights and property of the state." Taking a step back, the university policies do not eliminate users' expectations of privacy in their computers; instead they establish limited instances in which university administrators may access their computers to protect the university's systems. Thus, students had a reasonable expectation of privacy in information they transmitted over the university's network insofar as there was no announced monitoring policy.

Given the outcome of these court rulings, it is important for associations to be clear to their members and users as to what, if any, expectation of privacy is present when using the forum. Ideally, users should be informed monitoring will occur and, as a result, there is no expectation of privacy. Further, associations should always work to ensure they are in compliance with the privacy policies they communicate to members.

Publication on Social Networking Sites

Moreno et al. v. Hanford Sentinel, Inc., et al., F054138, slip op. 09 C.D.O.S. 4208 (Cal. App. 5th Dist. April 2, 2009) develops the idea that there is no expectation of privacy when material is posted on third-party social networking websites, in this case, Myspace.com. The plaintiff was a young woman from Coalinga, California, who posted on her MySpace page "An Ode to Coalinga," a narrative containing extremely negative comments about the town and its residents. During the six days that the ode was posted on her MySpace page, the principal of Coalinga high school discovered it and sent it to his friend, the editor of the local newspaper, who republished it as a "Letter to the Editor." The author and her family received death threats and a shot was fired at the family home, forcing the family to move out of Coalinga. The plaintiff publicized her opinions about Coalinga by posting the ode on Myspace.com, a hugely popular internet site. Cynthia's affirmative act made her article available to any person with a computer and thus opened it to the public eye. Under these circumstances, no reasonable person would have had an expectation of privacy regarding the published material. The Court factored the wide popularity of the website into its opinion.

Given the implications of *Moreno,* associations should advise members who want to start a group or submit their own postings on third-party social networking sites that they will not have an expectation of privacy in the material they submit. Furthermore, it is a good idea to provide notice to third parties that the communication is privileged, proprietary, or confidential. Another consideration would be to make the communication password protected or encrypted (Jonathan Bick, "Existing Internet Laws Reduce Constitutional Protections," Internet Law & Strategy, May 2009).

The Electronic Communications Privacy Act of 1986 (ECPA), 18 U.S.C. §§ 2510-2521, 2701-2711, 3121-3127 (2006) extends government restrictions on wire taps from telephone calls to include transmissions of electronic data by computer. However, the ECPA only protects wire, oral, and electronic communications *while in transit.* Internet communication technology and protocols mandate that internet messages stop and be stored multiple times en route, thus eliminating the protections afforded by the ECPA to internet communication.

Wikis

By their very nature, wikis are user content regarding a particular industry term. Users are typically invited to contribute their own definitions and comments to the current definitions. Because wikis are created and edited by industry peers, they can be very useful tools for communicating key industry concepts. Wikis can, however, communicate inaccurate or incomplete information. As such, readers should be cautioned that the opinions expressed as part of any wiki are those of the contributor and are not those of the association; therefore, the association is not responsible for any damages as a result of the wiki.

Conclusion

Associations and nonprofits can protect themselves and their members by monitoring their own listservers and bulletin boards according to their own terms of use. Likewise, associations should warn their members that extensive participation in third-party social media websites may cause damage to the participants and to the association as a whole. So when it comes to Web 2.0, associations should implement policies, user agreements, and disclaimers to minimize their risk of liability.

About the Authors

Barbara F. Dunn, Esq. is an attorney and partner in the St. Louis office of Howe & Hutton, Ltd. She can be reached at (636) 256-3351 or bfd@howehutton.com.

Nathan J. Breen is an attorney and partner in the Chicago office of Howe & Hutton, Ltd. He can be reached at (312) 263-3001 or njb@howehutton.com.

Joshua W. Peterson is an attorney in the Chicago office of Howe & Hutton, Ltd. He can be reached at (312) 263-3001 or jwp@howehutton.com.

CHAPTER 8

Public Versus Private Social Networks—An Either/Or Proposition?

The rapid adoption of social networking as both a personal communication vehicle as well as a bona fide business practice has spawned a debate over what type of social network reigns supreme. The debate revolves around the superiority of public versus private social networks. This chapter discusses each in turn, providing definitions, benefits, and challenges. Organizations that wish to strategically employ social media tools to drive business value use the combined force of public and private social networks to maximize awareness of their unique value proposition.

Public Social Networks

Public social networks are those websites which are available to any user of the web and contain software applications that allow an individual to directly find, connect, and communicate with other individuals without the oversight or stewardship of a particular organization. The purpose of a public social network is to gather as many individuals together as possible. Neither the purpose of joining nor the activities undertaken by users are of importance to the company that offers the public social network.

Typically, the revenue model of public social networks revolves around advertising. The goal is to obtain enough people in one place so that the advertising corporations can put offers in front of individuals with the hope of creating demand for their particular product or service. In this way, the public social network is not innovative; it is just a new communication channel and can find its place next to TV, billboards, and the WWW organizational website.

The Value of Interaction

What is innovative about public social networks is that there is now a "star effect" that had never before existed. Because of the sheer number of users, public networks have the ability to make individuals feel famous, since they can promote themselves on a world stage simply through their interactions with the site.

Little to no emphasis is put on the value of interactions or contributions to the site. Uploading your image carries the same value as uploading your doctoral dissertation; "poking" people has the same value as recommending a colleague, and so forth. The user experience focuses on contributing information, and the value derived is strictly psychological, based on the emotional response users have with their own inputted content and the reactions of others to it.

Examples of Public Networks

Public networks have widespread recognition and usage. These Web 2.0 networks roughly fall into the following categories under the umbrella of what is considered social media:

Social Media Public Networks

While technically the term "social media" refers to the entire body of tools, applications, and techniques within the discipline of online user communications, the term is most commonly heard connected with public networking sites that offer videos, audio, and picture-sharing capabilities. The most well-known social media sites include the video-sharing giant YouTube and a multitude of picture-sharing sites such as Flickr.

Social Networking Public Sites

Like social media sites, many social networking sites offer similar capabilities with user constructs that have become standard best practice.

For example, the majority of social networking sites work off a standard model that requires the user to create a profile—another name for a user account that contains personal information—to participate in website activities.

Typically, the user's profile includes the ability to add a picture, demographic or psychographic information, and personal thoughts or anecdotes to allow the users to describe themselves to the website community. Users may then participate by finding other users through search directories or another automatching capability that matches descriptive criteria included in user profiles. This process of self-directed or autofinding of like-minded individuals is typically called "friending" or "connecting" and is one of the biggest benefits touted by social networking sites.

The rationale behind connecting users is that like-minded users will come together online to communicate or collaborate around a common interest or topic and in so doing, create "social artifacts." Social artifacts are often also called "user-generated content" and really mean that users leave a virtual paper trail in the form of online content. In this case, content takes a broad definition and may include uploaded documents, presentations, videos, audio files, comments, rankings, voting, and blog entries.

The premise behind social networking sites is that they are a cost-effective way to connect people who share common interests or pursuits in order to efficiently communicate and incite some sort of action within the group. The pivotal questions in social networking sites become who is influencing the desired action and what the desired action is that the social networking site is spurring its population to undertake.

To answer these questions, it is critical to understand the business model that drives providers of public social networking sites. The most well-known public social networking sites are Facebook and LinkedIn. While each social network has its own target market, the business model is the same regardless of user population. The goal of each of these for-profit companies is the same: to drive as many users onto the site and gather as much information about each as possible.

Each of the sites uses sophisticated techniques to create a user experience where users feel that they are deriving value from the "free" use of their tool sets and are rewarded for entering copious amounts of personal information. LinkedIn, for example, uses a status bar to measure the completeness of your profile. This seemingly simple mechanism creates a desire in people to see the status bar at 100 percent complete, driving people to input more and more information. Facebook includes a laundry list of pre-defined categories that intuitively cause people to understand that they should fill out all of the fields, even those not required.

Public social networking sites are masters at creating the perception of value and the impression that the companies are providing these connection tools from an altruistic attitude. While this may be the case, it is a secondary driver in the public social networking companies' business model. Their first concern is to raise revenue through advertising sales. They are motivated to keep improving their websites to drive ever more data collection from their users so that this, in turn, can be turned into business intelligence that is highly valuable to prospective advertisers. Not surprisingly, public social networks do not highlight to users the fact that their business model is to collect user data in order to turn it into a saleable good to advertisers that can then more effectively market their products and services into more qualified, highly-targeted populations.

Blogging, Microblogging, and Vlogging Social Sites

Social media includes an entire set of website applications that allow for individuals or organizations to create and distribute online content for either a small fee or in exchange for providing personal information to use their service. Blogging is the term used for writing and publishing content online in a diary-entry format. Well-known providers of blogging software include Blogger, TypePad, and WordPress.

While blogging typically allows the user to post as much content as possible with no limit on the number of words or characters used, microblogging sets a limit on the number of words that can be published and distributed for any one post. Twitter is the most famous of micro-blogging platforms that limits the user to 140 characters per post. The primary driver behind Twitter is to provide one-to-many quick updates that cut down the time delay between message sender and message recipients. Vlogging is just another type of blog, but instead of using words, the author provides their commentary through use of recorded video.

The usefulness of blogging and microblogging tools relies on the premise that someone is consuming the information that is being generated. While having a content creation and delivery platform readily available to any person is appealing, the issue becomes how to effectively raise awareness of the existence of an individual user or organization's blog and get people to "follow" the published thoughts. Many organizations and individuals are open to the idea of using a more efficient content and delivery platform but struggle with finding like-minded people who are interested in similar topics or care about the same issues.

Social Bookmarking Websites

Another type of social media is roughly defined as "social bookmarking" websites. Like the other categories, there are many examples of these websites, but the basic premise behind each is the same: Allow users to specify a preference toward a particular website or content item, categorize and store the preference, and then, optionally, share the preference with other system users. Examples of this type of social media include sites such as Digg, Reddit, and Delicious.

The main premise of this kind of website is that the sheer amount of information now available to people through the internet is too vast for any one user to successfully navigate. Instead, if users band together and freely share their internet findings, individuals who share common interests or concerns may more easily learn or identify useful information from the collective wisdom of groups to which they "belong" through virtue of their shared interest or concern. This premise underlies all the social media sites and is the defining shared value of social media initiatives.

Benefits of Public Networks

Today's social networks offer a multitude of benefits. The most readily apparent is the availability of social networking tools and the incredible awareness within mainstream society of the existence of public networking tools. The promised benefits of social networking helped drive this widespread adoption, creating an environment in which everyone is aware, ready, and in a learning mindset about how to use these new tools. The main questions for companies that wish to use social networks competitively are, "Who will be the teacher?" and, "How will the tools be used?"

The company that can harness the message and method is the company that will be able to deliver real business benefits to its constituency. To this end, many organizations tend to immediately see that public networks are going to offer them the easiest path to this goal and the benefits that are readily apparent are extremely enticing, the first one being the apparently free usage.

No Usage Fees for End Users

Public networks such as LinkedIn, Plaxo, Facebook, Twitter, and social bookmarking sites do not require users to pay any sort of usage fee. Instead, fees are extracted from advertising and product placement opportunities. Public networks are based on a business model that is able to charge premium rates for advertising and product placement based on the number of people that comprise the network. The public network's incentive, therefore, is to drive as many people into public networks as possible to drive the numbers of ad impressions promised to advertisers and sponsors.

Level Playing Field Due to Equal Access to Sophisticated Website Functionality

The main benefit for organizations is that they, too, can participate in this public social sphere by signing up their organization or group just like an individual would. This organizational end user enjoys all the same features and functionality (sometimes even more) as individuals without incurring any use charges. Organizations can strategically view public networks as a new low-cost communication channel that can be used to increase awareness and drive demand while keeping, or even decreasing, their cost-of-sales ratio.

Public networking sites allow organizations of any size or technical sophistication to offer the latest software tools while bypassing the cost of development, acquisition, or management of the software itself. Organizations often find, however, that the total cost of ownership in using public networks is not zero dollars because the networks need to be nurtured and maintained by staff. The amount of staff is really dictated by the size of the community, size of the organization, and engagement level of the community as a whole. For example, some medium/large associations or nonprofits are assigning one full-time employee to manage the organization's presence on public networks and communities.

Vehicle for Brand Awareness

Arguably one of the most appealing benefits of public social networks is their ability to serve as a communication delivery channel that can be used to increase brand awareness. Because of the number of people using public social networks, adding your organization or individuals associated with your organization to the public sphere increases the probability of your organization's being recognized. Getting your name and mission in front of as many people as possible increases your odds of recruiting new members or perhaps re-engaging past members.

Organizations are particularly keen on using public social networks as a way to increase brand awareness because they believe that they will be able to reach new markets or expand their penetration into particular member segments, such as young professionals. A tremendous number of nonprofit organizations (notably associations and technical societies) are witnessing the rapid aging and decline of their member populations due to retirement and are working to re-engineer their membership base for future generations. These organizations believe that social networks will help them to reach younger individuals and turn them into lifetime members.

Challenges of Public Networking Sites

While many of the public networking sites now offer various mechanisms to restrict access to groups or content, these options still do little to hide the fact that the sites are not under the control of the individual or organizational user. The chief challenge with public networking sites is that you are essentially borrowing another company's space to push your own message or create your own group. This type of social "squatting" may be of value in driving awareness of your organizational brand, but it does little from the standpoint of actually managing your brand.

Issues in Brand Management

Brand management is a particular challenge for several reasons. First, the environment in which the user interacts within public networks is outside your organization's control. You have no control over the advertisements that are shown and perhaps positioned next to your logo or in some way associated with your brand. For example, a Facebook page dedicated to animal rights might have a deer hunting ad on that same page. You also have zero control over what the overall environment looks like, how it behaves, or how it may change.

All these aspects are controlled by the public social networking company that provides the site. Your organization may easily fall victim to the elimination of certain features or functions on which you've come to rely. Just as consumers rarely get the chance to prevent a beloved product from being removed from the market, so with social networks, your organization is at the mercy of the public social networking companies' product marketing managers, who may or may not solicit the input of users of their websites.

User Data

Perhaps even more of a challenge than brand management is the inability to control, collect, or analyze user data that is generated and stored on public networking sites. This "member gold" is created each time an individual joins your organizational online group, mentions your organization, connects with other people who share common interests (and who could very well be prospective members or donors), or adds their own thoughts to a discussion topic pertinent to your organization's mission or industry.

Since the business model of the public networking site provider is to collect this very data, there is zero incentive for the provider to share this data with organizations. Should today's social media environment change, data extraction will certainly come with a sizable price tag. Organizations that rely solely on public social networking sites are losing their member intelligence every day that they aren't capturing and analyzing the engagement of their members.

A related challenge concerning user data lies in the disparate nature of public networks. Since public social networks are distinct entities that exist outside the organization's information management systems, the organization is in a double bind: The organization has no access to the data being generated about their members or prospective members and is therefore unable to generate any business intelligence from it; and because there is no access to this data, it can't be combined with the vast amounts of user data that any typical organization has spent years collecting and managing. Most nonprofit organizations have heavily invested in their information systems to ensure that their member and donor data are as rich as possible. Organizations spend considerable sums each year to maintain their systems and keep their data accurate and comprehensive.

A typical organization collects and uses not only member contact information but also member communication preferences, transaction data (product and service purchases, event attendance), demographic data, and psychographic data. An organization's membership management system is the true core of its body of knowledge; private social networks offer the capability of adding the piece that has always been missing—actual user behavior—to create the complete picture of a given individual. Unlike private social networks, public networks lack the ability to extract this behavioral data and so their usefulness is limited

Lack of Organizational and Structural Control

By virtue of the tools' being publicly available, all users of public social networks are equal and have equal access to the creation and management of groups, posting comments, starting discussions, and the like. This is highly problematic for organizations, as their main selling point is the ability to assemble, organize, and mobilize qualified people around a common cause.

Public social networks have now provided any given user the ability to create and manage an organization. This has led to the creation of multiple groups that are subsets of organizations or that have started without the consent or help of an existing authentic organization. Many nonprofits can point to the creation of a Facebook page or LinkedIn group that touts their name and includes individuals that have self-associated with the organization's name, all without the organization itself having been involved.

Organizations risk obsolescence if they fail to identify what differentiates their capacity and capability from that of an individual or group of individuals who purport to offer the same networking and communication exchange as the organization. This capability provided by public social networks is now driving many nonprofits to rethink their value proposition and outline what benefits they can provide to members that an online-only group cannot.

Private Social Networks

The first thing to define about private social networks is the term "private," which is somewhat of a misnomer. While the word "private" when used in software typically refers to a user's access levels, the meaning when connected with social networks suggests one that is controlled by the organization. As opposed to public networks that are typically the product of for-profit companies offering tools in exchange for personal data, private networks are the product of companies offering tools in exchange for subscription fees. Private social networks, therefore, consist of those social networks built on tools that are leased from software providers, but whose data, operations, and management are fully owned by the organization leasing the software.

The core tenet of public versus private networks is very different. In the public network, the organization is little more than a squatter—trying to gain through the use of borrowed tools offered in an unpredictable environment. In the private network, the organization is akin to a company renting office space in a managed building and eligible to receive the rights and protection offered through a binding legal contract.

What is interesting is how many organizations view public networks as free and private networks as cost-prohibitive. When viewed from a risk management standpoint, it becomes clear that the subscription fees required to lease stable software tools is a small cost to pay to house, protect, and collect the organization's data.

Private networks originate from a fundamentally different business model. In public networks, the software provider's business model centers on revenue generation from advertising. In private networks, the software provider's business model revolves around this concept of leasing virtual "office space."

Commercial realtors provide offices that contain cubicles, a kitchen, conference room, and furniture so that your labor force has a safe, consistent, and dependable environment in which to work. Private social networking companies are offering a space in the internet to provide your organization with the security, groups, blogs, discussion areas, and connectivity pieces to allow your labor force—in this case your members—a safe, consistent, and dependable environment in which to work. As an added bonus for today's virtual environment, the entire work product produced in this space is automatically stored and saved by the organization for use by members.

Basic Constructs of a Private Social Network

The following are basic constructs of a private network regardless of software provider.

Security

Private networks want to ensure that members of the social network are protected. Through use of permissions and security settings, users of the social network may be limited in terms of what they can access or in which ways they can participate within the system. For example, a user may have a security role of "member" (or "donor") with the ability to see a large variety of documents and make comments and add to the document collection but be unable to participate in a discussion that is reserved for "board members." In another example, a member may be allowed to view the proceedings of a board meeting but not have the permissions to actually engage in the conversation. These variations on who can do what allow the organization to set up workflow processes and address their transparency levels through security settings designed into private social networks.

Data Collection and Ownership

Private social networks track and collect all aspects of user behavior. From log in to page views to ratings, private social networks typically store all interaction points in a database along with the actual content generated by the user's interactions with the site itself and with others. This behavioral data is owned by the organization and software service providers should offer organizations a way to export and import this data should the need arise to find another software provider.

Social Networking Tools

One of the differentiators of private social networking software providers is the actual bundle of tools offered. Typically, the same types of social networking tools available in public networks are available for use in a private setting. This set of tools includes:

- the capabilities of connecting one user to another through a method of invitation or group assignment

- member search and categorization capabilities
- the ability to create and administer groups
- blogs
- wiki capabilities
- the ability to contribute content through uploading or commenting on content
- rating and ranking of content
- interactive discussion lists
- alert mechanisms including email and RSS feeds
- interoperable web parts that can be exported to other websites
- digital ribbons and recognition management
- community application integration

System Integration

Another major differentiator between private network providers is their ability to integrate the private network into your existing systems. The more tightly your private social network is integrated into your existing technology ecosystem, the less disruptive the experience will be for your system users and the more rapid the user adoption will be of the new social network. Savvy organizations seek software providers that offer the following capabilities:

- Single sign-on (SSO) to allow for one log in between your organization's various website properties and web applications
- Standardized data exchange routines with your organization's specific association management system (AMS), donor management system, or customer relationship management (CRM) system
- Web development capabilities that focus on database architecture and design and application development as opposed to web graphic and content design
- Legal partnerships with manufacturers of software systems used by your organization to ensure that integrations are standardized and supported by all of your system providers

Hosted Environment

As part of the lease fee for your private social network, your organization will receive a hosted environment in which your membership may collaborate and work. This hosted environment includes both the structure and the data integrity assurances that you would expect from a known premium website hosting provider. Organizations should look for software providers that use industry best practices in providing scalable hosting services with guaranteed levels of service. Private network providers typically offer the following elements in a hosted environment:

- Look and feel of the site that carries your organization's visual identity and not that of the private social network provider (This is also referred to as "white label networks.")
- Subdomain or domain that resolves to the private network, although typically private network providers do not become the domain registrar or domain host
- Database-driven web applications that are continuously improved through automated updates that do not require your organization to install or test new features
- Virtualized server environment that allows for redundancy, recovery, and data mobility
- Physical data server security in a facility designed for server hosting
- Managed services to oversee server operation and performance
- Cloud utilization to ensure deliver via a Content Delivery Network (CDN) to ensure high speed web pages to a global audience

Benefits of Private Social Networks

The key differentiator between public and private networks is the ability to gather and then analyze the data that reflects the behavior, relationships, and preferences of system users. While the ability to collect this data and combine it with user data already institutionalized within your organization's member management system is indeed a huge value for the organization, the true benefits of social networks are not in the data itself but in how the organization can use the data to improve its overall value proposition.

Private social networks are likely going to be the key service delivery platform for new value-driven member programs. The true benefits of a private social network result in transformative organizational offerings and operational methods including:

Brand Redefinition

Many organizations are realizing that they are in crisis; their value proposition does not seem to warrant the loyalty or response from their members enjoyed in the past. Cutting prices and discount offers do not generate the desired revenue or attendee numbers. The old stand-by answers of "networking" and "education" as the value of what organizations provide don't seem to be working anymore. What organizations are realizing is that we are moving into a new era and the post-industrial, member-based organization needs to change, but no one seems to be sure about what needs to change or how it should change.

Most member-based organizations were founded to support the rise of manufacturing-based industries. Organizations, therefore, have traditionally focused on management techniques of cost-cutting and controlled production and mass marketing techniques for sales and awareness. Member-based organizations served the membership through providing products and services that could be mass produced and mass marketed to all, but input into the production process was limited to the number of people to whom the organization could realistically listen—in fact, a very small number.

What social networks have done is radically increase an organization's ability to listen to its membership and, in so doing, offer the organization the ability to redefine its brand. Instead of being an organization that produces new products and services with the hope that the membership might adopt and buy what is offered, organizations using social networks are realizing that their brand can be established on the ability to listen and respond. Smart organizations are redefining their value proposition to what makes them different—what they do better than any other organization or group—is they give members a safe environment in which to communicate, collaborate, and receive positive recognition for their contributions.

This move toward establishing brand from the basis of facilitation as opposed to product origination is helpful for the organization. This allows the organization to re-establish itself as a flexible structure that can take in vast amounts of member input, aggregate and prove the demand for services and products, and then provide these to the membership. In many cases, what members truly are demanding is access to other members; the products they produce when thinking together are the output of a savvy organization's delivering on its value proposition to members. Social networks are allowing organizations to redefine their brand by moving them into the role of facilitator of member-to-member idea, product, and content creation.

Innovation

Once brand value shifts from a manufacturing perspective to a facilitation perspective, the environment for innovation is created. Organizations using private social networks are now in a position to provide a forum for idea generation, exchange, and cultivation. Offering a safe place where individuals may submit ideas, questions, challenges, and observations of their own and also consume submissions of others leads to further inquiry and investigation. This cycle of observation-to-inquiry leads to constructive discourse that is focused on finding new ways to solve problems and jointly identifying cause factors and coping methods for challenges faced by the collective whole.

Organizations using private social networks can offer "idea labs" and "future forums" whereby they invite and encourage members to document their perspectives on the current state of affairs and air their viewpoints about the future path of an issue, the industry, or their profession. Offering structured groups in which individuals are not only encouraged but also rewarded for thought leadership naturally creates more engaged members who take on a stewardship role in the organization's existence. These types of member-based forward-looking constructs offer individuals an easily recognizable value for their membership dollar and the creative nature of being forward-focused promotes excitement and energy in most member populations. Moreover, the fact that the ideas are generated together in a transparent environment leads to faster idea adoption and unification behind an idea, all of which lead to a stronger member population.

Product and Service Development Cycle

With a brand built on facilitation and an environment supportive of innovation, it is not surprising that social networking is perceived as a disruptive innovation which can significantly change the traditional product and service development cycle currently used by most organizations. If an organization is equipped to truly listen and evidence demand for products and services, it can modify or create new offerings that are wanted or needed by an identifiable segment of its member population or the majority of its membership.

Perhaps your organization sees that more people would like to benefit from the educational content offered at your conference, but the time or travel cost is too high to attend in person. Now that your conference is supported by a private social network, your organization might decide to sell a virtual conference pass that allows the virtual attendee access to not just the conference materials presented at the conference but also the actual conversation occurring around the materials.

In addition to new revenue, your organization is now creating new value to members and increasing the opportunities for engagement. The change in thinking from controlling situations to finding ways to increase the engagement in situations leads organizations to develop new products and services that benefit member-to-member interaction—and often provide real business impact to the organization.

Faster and More Successful Go-to-Market (GTM)

When an organization starts to provide products and services to answer quantifiable demand, there is little mystery about whether a product or service will be successful when it is released to the market. Private social networks provide an ideal conduit for not only listening but also responding to the needs of a member population. Organizations can shed their fear of bringing new offerings to their membership market and, instead, can spend more time focused on developing go-to-market (GTM) strategies that will minimize the time required for the majority of a population to exhibit adoption of the new product or service.

Through word-of-mouth, testimonials, endorsements, and ratings, private social networks offer a plethora of ways for members to not only try new products but also spread the word about the new offering. Smart organizations are realizing that social networks offer easy ways to find early adopter groups and focus groups that can test new products or services before introducing them to the general membership.

Organizations are using online communities to not only try out but advocate on the organization's behalf for other members to adopt a certain idea, method, or offering. Organizations are now seeing that social networks provide improved ways to maximize efficiency and minimize the risk of new product or service offerings while opening new ways to go to market through a partnership relationship with member advocates of the new product or service offering.

Lower Delivery Costs

Private social networks are, in fact, a new delivery platform for many of the products and services that you now offer but present distinct cost saving advantages due to their virtual nature. For example, if your organization now spends resources on the myriad of tasks needed to collect enough information to run a session-based conference, private social networks now offer a far more economical way to both collect and distribute content to the attendee base.

Private social networks lower delivery costs of content creation, distribution, storage, and retrieval. By allowing members to self-serve and to serve others, private social networks also often lower the delivery cost of customer/member support. When members are empowered to help each other, the organization can benefit through reallocating its staff time toward facilitation and member recognition and away from providing tactical one-on-one help to individual members.

Recruitment

Showcasing the fact that your social network is private can be a very effective recruitment tool. While the majority of the content in a private social network is truly private (i.e., a user must have the appropriate security assignment to view or modify the content), successful organizations also recognize that the very nature of a private community can be a key factor in creating demand for membership.

Much as the small signs that state "private driveway" or "members only" pique the interest and make one wonder what is inside, so, too, membership organizations can provide a hint of what lies within the private network. With a growing population of engaged members who are creating content, sharing ideas, and collaborating on projects, social networks provide organizations with hard evidence of the value of membership. Smart organizations highlight the interactions, provide appropriate recognition, and showcase the value of membership through highlighting various examples of member interaction and contributions. Simply providing a compelling community homepage that is open to the public and available for search engine indexing can often lead to greater exposure and incite demand for further inquiry into membership.

Loyalty-Based Retention

Private social networks provide organizations with new means to build loyalty programs designed to garner higher retention rates. Once a social network is installed and users begin to adopt, organizations may take on a facilitation and recognition role whereby they observe contributors and participants and reward their behavior. The majority of psychology work that investigates long-term change, points out that sustainable change is accomplished only through positive feedback. Social networks provide organizations with the opportunity to provide consistent praise and recognition to active participants economically and quickly. The effects are two-fold: Individuals who receive praise feel valued and more connected, and individuals who see others receive praise understand that their efforts will be appreciated should they contribute. The individual effect is ever-greater loyalty and involvement. The organizational effect is an ever-increasing positive feedback cycle that can be used to institute and direct change.

Legacy Creation

One of the biggest benefits for private social networks is that, in effect, your organization is implementing a perpetual knowledge bank that captures not only the documentation of the membership but also the conversations, interactions, and relationships among members. The entire social network becomes a living legacy of the membership organization and can be used as a way to establish and institute organizational legacy.

Think of the social network as an ever-growing time capsule of information created during specific time periods and surrounding specific topics of interest. In the future, your organization can look back at the historical conversations in a snapshot mode to use in benchmarking progress and as a way to provide context to decisions and direction. Additionally, organizations can begin to look at the interactions of the member population at the aggregate level to identify historical patterns and trends that can be used in decision making and strategic planning.

Challenges of Private Social Networks

Private social networks offer an extraordinary number of benefits to organizations, but they do pose new challenges. The majority of issues currently seen in private social networks arise because of the paradigm shift brought about by new social technologies that are disrupting traditional business processes and practices.

New Budgeting Approach

One of the largest shifts for organizations to make in using private social networks is in budgeting appropriately for the new initiative. Many organizations have yet to become familiar or comfortable with acquiring software on a subscription basis, known as Software as a Service, or SaaS.

Organizations are used to the typical software acquisition method that dictates that the application is either custom-built in-house or is acquired through a capital expenditure and amortized over multiple years. In the traditional model, organizations "own" the software license after the amortization period and typically, continue to pay a yearly fee to the software manufacturer for upgrades and basic support that is 20 percent to 30 percent of the original cost of the software.

SaaS models, instead, are based on monthly or yearly subscriptions that require an ongoing outlay of money to support the system and never confer ownership to the organization. This model typically requires the organization to switch its budgeting of software from a capital expenditure item to an operating expense item, with subscription fees budgeted into yearly operating expenses. Many organizations struggle with selling the idea of a perpetual new expense item because they fail to recognize that the year-over-year subscription cost is typically still less than the 30 percent license maintenance fees charged in the traditional software model.

Total Cost of Ownership

Few organizations really investigate the total cost of ownership (TCO) of a social network and, therefore, underestimate not only the cost but also the value. This inability to accurately assess TCO makes it difficult for organizations to adequately establish the value and assess return on investment (ROI) of the private social network.

Organizations that have successfully implemented private social networks know that software subscription fees are just one part of TCO and that human capital also must be expended to establish the network and drive members to adopt it. Social networks are not a member program that follows a "build it and they will come" methodology; the network either must be cultivated and overseen by a staff member or outsourced to a firm or consultant that offers expertise in community development and management.

Without a clear picture of TCO, organizations often establish unrealistic expectations and timeframes on which to assess ROI. It is imperative that organizations fully budget for and understand the efforts required to establish a private social network so that expectations are correctly communicated to staff, component leaders, and the general membership. Without accurate TCO buy-in, organizations are often setting themselves up for frustration and shifting the onus of the success of the network onto the membership's use of the software.

Organizational Behavior

Changing organizational behavior is an age-old challenge. While social networks bring new insight into the membership, they also require the organization to adapt to new ways of communicating and interacting with members. This need to adapt and find new ways to think and work with the social-networked membership distresses many organizations.

Where organizations once were the originators of all information, now they are just one source of content. Organizations sometimes struggle with accepting the new role of facilitation instead of content control. Social networks are inherently collaborative, based on reward and praise for contributions, as well as cross-functional. If these attributes conflict with the actual culture and structure of the organization, the social network will highlight the misalignments and require some aspect of change management.

Additionally, private social networks require stewardship on the part of the organization. Associations must appropriate resources, time, authentic interest, and support for the private social network to flourish. Organizations that struggle with focus, exhibit lack of discipline in staying the course for initiatives, or are quick to quit new initiatives if immediate success is not seen may find private social networks challenging because of lack of a supportive organizational culture.

Components often found in private social networks which are not usually present in public social networks:

I. Brand Considerations

- Control of visual identity
- Control of advertisements
- Control of positioning
- Control of structure and presentation of site

II. Knowledge Management Considerations

- Allows for export of user-generated content
- Allows for creative commons licensing
- Integrates with existing content management and other in-house systems

III. Technology Considerations

- Allows for single sign-on with your existing website(s)
- Integrates with your member/contact management systems
- Allows for data storage and retrieval
- Offers data extraction for reports and data mining
- Organization signs a service-level agreement that guarantees performance
- Organization owns the data both input by staff and created by users of the network
- Data structures that already exist in your systems may be leveraged to configure and manage your network

IV. Communication Considerations

- Different users can receive different messages based on security levels and permissions
- Communication between groups is archived and available even if users change roles

- Track metrics for actual communication uptake and action through site usage statistics
- Outbound emails and alerts carry your organization's visual identity

The Power of Two: Combining Private and Public

The fastest way to get real returns on your social networking endeavor—the point at which you will bypass your break-even point and start to make real gains—comes when the power of private and public networks are combined. While it may seem intuitive that if you use the two types of networks in combination greater awareness will occur, it is actually uncommon that organizations go into social networking projects focused on the interplay between public and private. Instead, most organizations identify with one or the other and, subsequently, do not make the desired headway in forming online communities.

Why Organizations View Public and Private Networks as an Either/Or Proposition

There are a number of reasons organizations do not first start with the framework of a combined public and private network landscape, including:

1. Scarcity Mindset

The majority of organizations come from a mindset of scarcity, the idea that resources are so few that new projects can only occur to the detriment of an existing project and that the only available resources are those that exist within the organizational staff. This mindset leads organizations to often approach new technologies and communication methods from a framework of fear. In this vein, organizations may choose to only adopt new communication methods after other organizations have provided a proven model or only after succumbing to prolonged duress created from negative member feedback.

Organizations with the scarcity mindset typically approach social networking from a perspective of "let's try just one thing at a time." This type of organization will invest time in either a public or a private network using the premise that if one works, they can venture on to trying another application. Unfortunately, in a world where multiple channels of communication are required, this is a faulty premise. Organizations need to retool and build from the premise that multitasking and multichannel communication are the norms if messages are going to be effectively sent and received.

2. Not Enough Time

Organizations often cite that there is simply not enough time to focus on both a public and private network. The premise again is that public and private networks are an either/or proposition and the organization has missed the fact that the combination of the two is what propels a user from awareness to adoption.

Organizations may feel pressure to use all the myriad of social networking tools now available and, therefore, use precious resources posting to Twitter, Facebook, LinkedIn, Yahoo! Groups, and on and on without any gauge on whether the time invested is worthwhile or any certainty that the social networks are working to achieve the desired goals of recruitment and retention. The result is that organizations feel overwhelmed, often either seeing an ebb/flow of effort or stopping their social networking efforts altogether.

What organizations fail to recognize is that they have been operating from a premise that the quantity of social networking posts is what will make their organization relevant. Organizations should instead focus on the quality that comes from a comprehensive plan; knowing what you are trying to accomplish and having a plan of execution to lead a user from awareness to adoption allows the organization to increase its efficiency in time spent posting to social networks. Once the user flow of demand is understood and a few techniques are adopted, organizations find that time does, in fact, exist to perform social networking tasks. The results begin to build upon themselves and organizations start to see that their network truly can influence user behavior.

3. Lack of Education and Experience

The third reason that so many organizations have difficulty in adopting a combined view of public and private networks was previously alluded to, but deserves to be further discussed: lack of education and experience. In many situations, social networks are not only a new product or service to be introduced into the organization's business practices but also an entirely new product that needs to be delivered to the membership. The issue arises because many organizations have not launched a new product category in decades and the skills, knowledge, and experience in a new product launch just do not exist in the organization.

To further complicate matters, little experience previously gained through new product introduction is relevant to a product launch in today's market. Any new products that were released to the general membership before the mass adoption of the internet and then before social networking faced a very different landscape than what marketers face today. New product introduction now requires a much more flexible, much faster, and far more comprehensive approach in the methods used to stimulate interest and adoption. The same staid, one-dimensional techniques previously used to communicate member benefits will not garner desired results.

Organizations are now beginning to understand that the skills of marketing—the ability to create demand and position, place, and price products—are needed to successfully launch and grow the new product category called social networking. Organizations face a challenge of deciding whether to try to build this organizational capacity internally or to outsource.

Many organizations have adopted a strategy of initially outsourcing the launch and growth portions of their social network to consultants while simultaneously building internal capacity to bring the work of social network management back in-house. The need for more education and experience is easily evidenced by the growing number of educational webinars, seminars, courses, and consultants that are promoting their ability to either educate or lead organizations through this capacity building.

Creating Demand Using the Combined Framework

Public networks, in this context, are used to raise awareness, pique interest, and tantalize users that share common characteristics with those of your members. Public networks entice users to learn more about the organization that can evidence loyalty and innovation. To put it in tactical terms, the purpose of posting to LinkedIn is not to give away information about what your membership is doing; it is to entice nonmembers to want to be part of the conversation to which they are currently not privy.

It is not imperative that you blanket all the world of social networking with your message; what is imperative is that the message itself creates the perception of unrealized value. This created need is what sparks people's interest and begins to prime them for recruitment. Combining interest with clear evidence that the organization values its current members by publicly recognizing them doubles the recruitment effect created when public networks are used to create the awareness of the existence of a vibrant private community.

Once a user converts into a member of the community, the combined framework now provides a doubled effect from the retention side. Instead of taking in a new member and quickly subsuming their identity, the social network instead celebrates their existence and raises awareness to both members and nonmembers that are outside the private community. This member recognition provides evidence to new members that they have joined a community that values their contributions and helps to build confidence that they are in a supportive environment. This combined feeling of comfort and support decreases any "joiner's remorse" the new member may experience and rapidly decreases the time required to turn a new member into an actively engaged member.

Delivering Value-Based Member Programs through Private Networks

The difference between buzz and real interest is that demand is created when you offer nonmembers a look into the value-based member programs that exist within your private social network. To be clear, it is not enough to post to public networks that you have a private network or that you have like-minded members; these messages do not convince and can be quickly discerned as "buzz" by today's savvy and sophisticated users.

The private social network is the ultimate repository of all member interaction, collaboration, and involvement in organizational affairs. It is also the conduit for organizations to deliver these programs and should be seen as the lowest cost delivery platform for value-based member programs. To this end, the private network needs to offer innovative value-based programs that allow members to get something new that is noteworthy; this new value is what can be communicated through the public networks to pique interest and drive demand for membership.

Member-Based Programs That Offer Real Value

New member-based programs that offer real value for the membership may include:

Content Repositories to Support Knowledge Communities

Organizations may decide to leverage content repository and collaboration functionality offered through private networks to house and stimulate further development within particular knowledge communities. A program may be built where volunteers steward the creation, collaboration, and categorization of knowledge in a given area in an effort to create a knowledge base that benefits the greater population or industry.

Directories

Private networks provide an ideal platform to deliver new value-based member directories that allow users to quickly identify and contact individuals who possess specific areas of expertise or experience. Taking the idea of connecting like-minded people to heart, organizations create new value-based programs through offering multiple interactive directories that seek to match people based on education, work experience, topical areas, interest areas, and other characteristics. Organizations create value for the membership by taking on the role of facilitator and enabling members to find each other more easily and through ever increasing new ways of categorizing and matching users together.

Discussions

Organizations have long delivered member value by allowing certain discussions to occur only among members. Private social networks build on this traditional member benefit by automatically archiving, categorizing, and linking back discussions to individual members so that thought patterns and interactions are preserved. Past communication methods allowed for value to be created only in the moment of the discussion and lasted only while a thread was active or before a digested email listing all posts was sent out via email. Today's private social network becomes the storehouse for capturing conversations and understanding both the context of the dialogue and the players within the dialogue, leading to greater understanding of both topics under discussion and the members themselves.

Innovation Groups

A new value-based member program that organizations can easily deliver through private social networks is that of innovation groups. These online communities combine individuals who are interested in shaping the future of the organization and seek to work together to envision new solutions or pathways for the organization. The organization itself takes on the role of facilitator and offers members the ability to self-select into areas where they wish to lend their voices in shaping the future direction of the organization. These groups offer a new spin on governance and provide a new voice to those who wish to lead and serve in nontraditional ways. Organizations benefit by being more inclusive, increasing the awareness and access to diverse opinions, and offering new avenues to gain different ways of thinking.

The organization facilitates the existence of online groups and ensures that the feedback is periodically collected, organized, and fed back to the online community for further analysis and assessment. The program ensures that the organization plays the role of steward for the group and does not let ideas die but ensures that organizational leaders are presented with the group's input. Innovation group programs are a partnership between members and organizational staff, with each playing a part: members interacting and staff organizing and identifying trends and patterns in the aggregate.

Idea Labs

Similar in many ways to innovation groups, idea labs are based on having your organization provide an environment and online culture that promotes creativity and brainstorming. Idea labs are online areas where members can go to put forward ideas and ask for help in testing new ideas, experimenting and reporting back on findings of new ideas in action, and analyzing ideas by looking for new models and modes of operation. The constructs of idea labs may vary. They may be a discussion group centered on brainstorming solutions for a common problem, or they may be as involved as offering an entire website dedicated to the pursuit of new solutions.

Regardless of the actual software features and functions that power an idea lab, the idea stays the same: Create an online community that focuses on the germination and cultivation of new ways of doing things. The organization's role is one of stewardship. Through ensuring that the environment is safe and set up for creative interaction, full of positive feedback and recognition, and populated with a cross-section of members that represent diversity and varied disciplines to help boost cross-pollination of ideas, organizations play an important role that members can easily understand and appreciate.

Moreover, organizations can shed the burden of being the originator of new ideas and, instead, take on the far more appreciated role of providing an environment that allows for idea creation. Ridding the organization and the staff from the onus of idea creation and ownership and placing it back into the hands of the membership where it rightly belongs is one of the best ways an organization can free up valuable resources, reduce the stress on staff, and set itself up for success.

Idea labs are often positive fonts of interactivity and knowledge sharing that lead to additional positive outcomes. Members who engage in idea labs may decide to further collaborate on articles, write papers together, present at a conference together, put together pilot projects, start a new investigation, or use members as sounding boards or advisors. In any case, the collegial feel and atmosphere that are created, combined with the energy that ensues from creative problem solving, work to build a spirit of camaraderie and group-based idea ownership.

The energy and ideas that issue from idea labs can be turned around to fuel recognition programs and retention programs. Through highlighting snippets of idea lab goings-on in public social networks, organizations may use their new value-based member programs to come full-circle and fully recognize the positive feedback cycle between demand creation and program delivery. This cycle, again, is only fully functional and mutually reinforcing when public and private networks are combined and not treated as mutually exclusive entities.

Summary

With so many social networking tools now available for organizational use, it is more important than ever that organizations stop seeing public and private networks as an either/or proposition. Through focusing on a public social network without regard for the data and intellectual property that the organization forfeits or focusing solely on a private social network that does little to spur the positive demand creation cycle needed to keep members energized and interest new prospects, organizations are missing the full opportunity afforded by social media.

Organizations should focus their social media strategies on choosing the right combination of public and private social networks to create a dynamic relationship between members and nonmembers, demand creation and program delivery, and organizational staff and the membership itself. Sophisticated organizations are now focused on the interplay between public and private social networks and working to set up a system that provides a win-win situation to all participants. This new way of both communicating and delivering value-based member programs allows the organization not just to retain but also to grow its relevance and to deliver on its organizational goals and mission.

CHAPTER 9

The Relationship between Social Networking and Search Engines

Nobody really knows anything for sure about search engine optimization (SEO). It's all trial and error against the search algorithms, which are constantly changing, making it difficult to guarantee high placement in the search engine results pages (SERPs). The exponential growth in the social web has confirmed much of what we previously perceived to be true and enlightened us with new SEO principles.

SEO Basics

Before we dive into how to leverage the social web to improve your site's search engine performance, let's cover some of the basics for SEO.

Title Bar

Check the title bar of your page. The title bar is the blue bar (in Microsoft Internet Explorer) at the very top of your browser above the BACK button and above the "File" menu item. Check what you have displayed there. This is the most important part of your page optimization and the easiest to address. The title can be up to about 70 characters in length and should contain your top keywords. In the following example, ASAE's title bar shows "ASAE & The Center for Association Leadership."

The title bar not only influences your positioning in the search results, but it is also the heading that appears in the SERPs as well as the heading which will appear in someone's favorites after they click "Add to Favorites" or "Bookmark." If your title bar just says "Home" or "Welcome," people might not know immediately what the site is about. For your home page, try using the full name of the organization with the acronym (if applicable) and perhaps one or two keywords if you have room. (Remember the 70 character limit).

Header Tags

Pay attention to the H1, H2, and H3 tags. These should all contain variations of your top keywords. These tags are basically the headlines and sub-headlines on your pages. Try to repeat your most important keywords in subheadings multiple times if possible to increase keyword density.

Alt Tags

Make sure you use keywords in the alternative text description for images. The combinations of title, image, and header tags are top factors used by the search engines (in combination with inbound links). This is also necessary for accessibility reasons (e.g., for screen readers for the visually impaired).

Directory Submissions

Make sure your website is listed in the main directories (e.g., DMOZ.org, Yahoo and MSN). Google regularly imports the DMOZ directory. You cannot submit your site directly to the Google directory. Instead, you have to get it into the DMOZ directory and allow it to filter to the Google directory by virtue of one of their regular imports. Yahoo and MSN process your submissions for being listed in their directory faster than DMOZ, which is run by volunteers. One word of caution on your DMOZ submission: Be patient. Don't resubmit your submission to DMOZ in an effort to speed up the process because that will move you to the bottom of the queue again.

Link Love

The easiest way to understand link love is by thinking of something very different, such as webpages that you've added to your favorites. When you bookmark a page (add to your favorites), it is fair to assume the webpage has some significance for you. The question, from a programming perspective, is would it make sense to interpret the act of adding a webpage to your favorites as a vote of confidence for the web page and ultimately the domain name itself?

Google and the other search engines look at links from one website to another in a similar fashion. Because you've added a link to a specific webpage, the search engines see it as a vote of confidence for that page. When looking from a holistic perspective, search engines are allowed to calculate how many pages have a link to a specific webpage and ultimately the site which it belongs to. The more links there are to specific pages, the more the perceived value of that page.

When linking to a page, avoid linking the actual web address such as www.higherlogic.com as well as generic words such as "click here." The reason for this is that the search engines look at the words that are linked and then associate these with your site. Using Higher Logic as an example, a better way of linking to the site would be by saying something like "Higher Logic provides social media software for associations and nonprofits." In this example, if "social media software for associations" was linked but the rest was not, this would tell the search engines that this phrase and the individual keywords are relevant to this specific website. Conversely linking the words "click here" provides little to no value to the search engines.

Don't bother with link exchanges. Have you ever received an email asking for you to link to a website and in return they will link back to you? The problem with this approach is that the search engines are a little smarter than this, and by linking to each other you are effectively cancelling each other's link love. Link love is the value which you pass from one page to another purely by virtue of a link.

Search Engine Site Profiling

If a search engine sees your website as one of value (based on the number of links to it and other key attributes), then your site likely will appear high in the search engines for specific words or phrases. But what words and phrases? The search engines look to see what pages have links to your site and then compares the key words of your site and other websites which are linking to you, and from this, they essentially build a profile about your site. They know what your site is about and, more importantly, what it is relevant to. A higher placement in the search engines means more traffic to your site, and it will drive visitors/prospects and, ultimately, engagement to your site.

Bloggers Give Love

Bloggers are a key source of link love. Any mature blogger will blog about content on other sites (even if they are just points of reference for source material). When a blog is created about content posted elsewhere on the web, the blogger would typically link keywords or phrases to the blog they are writing about. This is extremely valuable to bloggers because every link means potentially a higher placement in the organic (natural) search results, which in itself will mean more traffic and potentially more readers of your content.

Leverage Partners

In an ideal world, you would never have any need to ask someone to link to you since they would do it simply because they value your website. However, there are many complementary, noncompeting sites that simply don't link. Link solicitation could be a full-time job and often is for many companies, but fortunately for associations and nonprofits, other websites will likely link to your site anyway as a useful resource or to announce they are members. Use the power of your brand to effectively push people to link to you. Create a "Proud Member of XYZ" logo that links to your website using your key phrase or tag line under the logo.

Quality Not Quantity

Remember it's not the quantity of the links; it's the quality. For example, if you have five pages linked to you from pages that have a high page rank (PR) value and have relevant content on the source pages (with few other outbound links on the same page), this is better than having several hundred links to you from pages with low PR values.

Outbound Links

Don't link to just anyone. Outbound links that go to dead pages can work against your organizational ranking. Use a tool like weblinkvalidator.com, which can find any broken link in your entire site as well as identify slow and poorly formatted pages.

Unique Content

When a search engine looks at a website and its respective webpages, one of the first things it tries to figure out is how unique the content is. In other words, is this site the source of unique content, or is it a site which has syndicated content from the source, or worse, a spam site designed to induce click through arbitrage?

HP Printer Example

To give a simple example of this, let's look at a for-profit example. Consider a manufacturer of a popular product such as the HP Laserjet III printer. HP put together very specific documentation, including a description of the product itself. The problem is that HP sells its printers through thousands of different reseller websites, most of which have the same description HP has provided them. So when users do a search for this particular printer, the last thing they want is to be taken to thousands of sites with identical content.

To get around this issue, the search engines try to identify the source of the information by noting the date/time the content was first discovered and how valuable the potential source site is (from external links to it). So if HP is the top search engine hit, what else will show below it? Usually these are sites that contain the right keywords based on other unique content that end users have provided via ratings, reviews, and comments. Often the HP standard printer description can be in the page as well, but since it has been wrapped around unique, user-generated content (UGC), the ratio of unique to non-unique content is reduced, which in turn causes the page to score more highly.

Unique Content and the Relevance to the Social Web

So what has this got to do with the social web? The social web is based mostly on user-generated content (UGC). Blogs by themselves are usually unique, and the comments and reviews which they attract are almost always unique. Combine the unique nature of the UGC with the links which the unique content may generate and you have search engine influence.

Leverage Volunteer-Created Content

Consider ways in which you can use the tremendous value of the unique content your discussion groups/forums/blogs are generating while retaining member benefits and protecting privacy. Consider a typical discussion group that might generate 20 messages per day, five days per week, and has been running for the last three years. 20 messages × 5 days × 52 weeks × 3 years = 15,600 messages with what is almost always unique content. Consider how many key phrases there are which could easily be matched to user searches within Google.

The traditional concern about displaying members-only content is that by giving away the content, there is one less reason for someone to become a member. If this is the case, try thinking creatively. For example, when you look at what is valuable in a discussion group posting, it is often the initial posting plus the responses. Perhaps consider opening the initial postings to the search engines with maybe the first line of each response with a link to become a member to view all the responses. In this example, you are still exposing a significant amount of UGC to the search engines which should help attract the long end of the tail in terms of search words and phrases.

Regular Updates

It's not enough to have unique content; the content also should be fresh. If Google finds two pages which score identically for specific keywords, which one will appear higher in the search results? The one which has been most recently updated with new, unique content will appear higher. Many associations and nonprofits have rested on their laurels knowing they are the number-one result for the most popular keyword(s) that represent their industry or interest. Some of these, however, are now finding they have been unexpectedly dislodged from their perch by one or more popular social media sites that have deliberately or accidentally scored well against that specific key phrase.

For example, a competitor to your nonprofit might be a typical blogger whose home page contains the latest blogs. Once enough new blogs have been posted, the older blogs move down the page. Finally the older blogs will be removed from the home page and put into a structured archive. Each blog will then be located at its own Permalink (permanent URL). The result is that the home page remains fresh with content and the comments and reviews that are added to the page, aid the perception of regular updates and uniqueness of content.

How to Leverage Dynamic Content

Nonprofits need to reinvent their websites to leverage user-generated content to ensure it is more dynamic. For an association, the latest blogs should not be just the staff-written blogs but also member-created blogs. Members or donors could have blogs attached to their profiles and all blogs could be wrapped up into a "blogroll," which is displayed as the "Latest Blogs" on the home page.

For example, see how the Society for Corporate Compliance and Ethics (SCCE) uses dynamic content on its community home page: http://community.corporatecompliance.org. SCCE places its members' recent blogs, discussion group postings, and library documents prominently on their home page.

The home page of a site is normally the most highly rated, and if it receives regular updates (latest blogs or discussion groups, for example), then this helps meet the "regular updates" requirement of the search engines.

User Generated Content (UGC) versus Organizational Generated Content (OGC)

For many years, the nonprofit information dissemination model has centered on the distribution of content written and reviewed by individuals working for or affiliated with the organization. The rise of web tools such as blogs and social media sites that have lowered the technological barriers to the distribution of content online has resulted in an explosion in the amount of user-generated content. Organizations that leverage this content and serve as cultivators and curators of conversations can better engage and activate their networks. This is a new model of content review that cannot follow the old model of copy approval.

In instances such as these, organizations don't control the conversation so much as leverage it. An organization can't be everywhere, but it can participate successfully with a keen focus on establishing a listening post, quickly identifying high quality contributions from others and re-sharing, and cultivating those who are consistent in their quality. This need for monitoring and being the first to respond, applaud, or clarify is a new way of behaving for many organizations whose publishing model includes onerous review and approval processes. But making the shift is critical to activating a network toward your issue goals.

There are many platforms through which nonprofits can aggregate and redistribute content related to their issue areas. These include:

- Public online communities (Facebook fan pages, LinkedIn Groups)
- Private online communities ("white label" social networks)
- Microblogging platforms (Twitter)
- Link aggregators (Digg, Delicious)
- Multimedia sharing sites (Flickr, YouTube)
- Blogs

Some organizations rely on user-generated content for specific campaigns. In 2009, the National Trust for Historic Preservation launched "This Place Matters," a photo contest to bring attention and awareness to historic preservation issues. Visitors were encouraged to take a picture of a person holding a "This Place Matters" sign in front of a place that they wished to honor. The photos were uploaded to Flickr and then voted on by other users.

Nonprofits that aggregate and redistribute content are of great value in today's information-overload world of social media. Rather than following 25 separate environmentalists on Twitter, people can turn to a trusted organization, such as The Nature Conservancy (TNC), to highlight and comment on the most important or relevant content. In an interview with *The NonProfit Times* published on February 1, 2010, Amy Ganderson, online marketing manager for The Nature Conservancy, notes that only one out of every seven tweets are about TNC, and the bulk of what they cover is what other people are doing and discussing.

The fact remains that as the barriers to contribute user-generated content to websites drops to negligible, it has become increasingly difficult to keep up with what is truly important and relevant. This can lead to social network burnout and abandonment. The true value of an issue-based organization is in its ability to filter relevant, high quality information and provide context and added value (analysis) to user-generated content.

Tools and Techniques to Help with Your Social SEO

Using Google as the example search engine, here are four top tips to help you with your social media endeavors.

Set Up a Google Webmaster Tools Account

You can set up an account at www.google.com/webmastertools. Google offers a tremendous set of tools that you can use to determine how you are doing in the search engines. For example, it will tell you about things that score negatively in the search engines, such as which pages are slow to load or have broken links and nonexistent pages that people are linking to.

Identify Key Words That Are Already Scoring Highly

The tools will also show you keywords that it finds relevant to your site as well as search terms and phrases that have scored highly and in what position for your site. If you want to go a little deeper to understand how much visibility your site is getting, you can see which terms and phrases your site is scoring highly for specific countries. This is important because the search indexes perform differently in different countries. For example, if your site is optimized for a specific phrase and it appears at the top of the search engines when searching Google in the United States, it may be several pages lower in European results.

Identify Who Is Linking to Your Site

Of particular importance to bloggers is the ability to see "Links to your site." This allows you to view all the domains and webpages that are linking to your website. Often bloggers can blog about your content, but you may not be aware of it. Since they may not mention any keywords for which you have set up alerts, it is easy to miss these new sources of exposure. If someone has taken the time to link to your site, then you should know what they are talking about and why they have mentioned (linked to) you.

Create a Sitemap File and Submit to the Search Engines

The search engines also allow webmasters to submit sitemaps. A sitemap is a compressed XML file that contains every page of your site about which you wish them to be aware. It is simply a long list of web addresses that is generated by one of many sitemap generator tools. The sitemap should run every 24 hours looking for new pages on your site and will automatically notify Google when it has finished compiling the information. Google then downloads the sitemap and is easily able to index every page in the sitemaps file (even if there is no link to it from within the site). Beware of indexing member only or content sensitive pages. To learn more about sitemaps files, see http://www.sitemaps.org/.

The search engines use something called "bots" to crawl the web. These are tiny programs which are designed to crawl and index web pages. The sitemap tools are particularly useful if you have pages with large graphics or that are slow to load for other reasons. Where a Google bot might normally give up and move on to the next website, now it can just ignore that page and jump to the next link instead of giving up entirely.

Other Webmaster Tools

The webmaster tools have many other uses, including identifying problems and recommending solutions to the HTML that your page is composed of as well as any meta information that the site might contain. For more information about this or to set up a free account, go to www.google.com/webmastertools.

Setup a Google Analytics Account

Google analytics is one of the most brilliant tools that social media experts can leverage. This free tool gives you tremendous insight into your web presence by logging traffic and visitation to your website. By simply embedding a very small piece of code in the template of your website (so it is on every page), Google is notified whenever anyone visits that page.

Google will record and track demographics such as where the person came from (a search engine or direct link), how long they stayed on the page, which page they clicked through to, and other general information such as how long they stayed on your site and how many pages they visited. The tools provide much more information than this, but this gives you an idea of the power, especially when you run cross-referencing ad hoc reports to determine levels of engagement.

To setup an analytics account, go to http://www.google.com/analytics.

Track Your Performance Using Page Rank

There are many ways to track your performance using analytics. One lesser known method of measuring your performance is through Google's Page Ranking Technology. This is a value between 0 and 10 which Google assigns every page on the web. You can see more about this technology at http://www.google.com/corporate/tech.html.

Google offers a free search toolbar that, once installed, allows you to see the page ranking (PR) it has assigned to any page you visit. (Go to options in the Google Toolbar to enable this feature.) While the PR value is only one of many factors that affect the SERPs, it is also an indicator of how valuable Google sees your pages as being. Google's PR algorithm has many factors; one of them is the number of inbound links to your site combined with the relevance and value of the content (not just in your site, but on the entire web). Track your PR rankings for your entire site over a period of time. Until recently, Google offered a way to view the most highly ranked pages in your site via its webmaster tools. However, Google has now removed this feature, so the only way to identify your page rank is by going to the specific page and viewing the PR on the Google toolbar.

Introduction to SitePRTracker

In 2006, I built a tool to help measure page rank to get around this problem. The tool is called SitePRTracker. It will crawl your website and grab the page ranking of every page of your site and will then provide average counts that you can track over time. It will also tell you how many pages have what page rank. For example, you might have 1,000 pages with a page rank of 2 and 400 pages with a page rank of 3 and so on. The Google search quality teams constantly try to remove emphasis of the page rank and ask webmasters to focus on the quality of their content instead. While this may be a good thing, if the page rank does what it is supposed to do (tells you the value Google finds any specific page), then the page rank is valuable in that it will give you feedback about how well you're doing. You can download a free copy of SitePRTracker at http://bit.ly/sitePRTracker

Once you start using a tool like this, you can then find out which of your blogs or other user-generated content has scored the highest page rank.

Identify and Remove Duplicate Content

A simple mistake which many webmasters make is to allow duplicate content within their site. Search engines really frown on duplicate content.

How to Identify Duplicate Content

In 2005, I created a website to help webmasters identify and deal with duplicate content. The website is free and can be found at www.CopyTester.com. Take some content from your website that you believe to be unique and copy and paste it into the home page of CopyTester.com. Then click on Evaluate and the system will analyze every word of every sentence and try to identify how unique each sentence is, and if there are copies, and it will tell you which sites the copied content falls under. Once it has finished analyzing, it will score the value of the content based on its uniqueness.

To really test this, try taking content from a page that is likely to have been copied, such as some content from your news archive or member benefits section. You'll likely be surprised at how many websites manually or programmatically copy content.

Mistakes That Create Duplicate Content Penalties

A few common mistakes that are easy to fix involve the domain name of the site and different views of the content, such as printable versions.

Domain Names

If your website URL is www.higherlogic.com, what happens when you visit just higherlogic.com (without the www)? One of three things typically will happen:

- You'll get a "page not found" error.
- Duplicate websites (the main website will display and the URL will remain just higherlogic.com)
- Permanent redirect (the main website will display and the URL will change to www.higherlogic.com)

Page Not Found

It's best to allow for both the www and non-www version to work, so this needs to be fixed by adding a redirect to your server.

Duplicate Websites

This is really the problem child of the three scenarios. If you allow the non-www to operate just like the www, then Google sees this as a different domain (which it is) and, therefore, treats it like a different website. This means that there exists an exact copy of your website and all its related content. This copy will then compete with your main www site, while trying to claim "source" status of any and all content on its respective website.

Permanent Redirect

As long as you have set a "Permanent Redirect" header from the one domain to the other, this is a good approach. If you Google "check site headers," you will find tools, such as seoconsultants.com, that will tell you if the higherlogic.com domain is returning the correct header value. When you enter higherlogic.com and click on search, the result should show that the page has a permanent redirect that points to www.higherlogic.com.

In addition to setting the permanent redirect, you can also log into your Google Webmaster Tools account, where there is an option to tell Google to treat both domains as the same website. Of course, this works for only Google, so applying the permanent redirect is still important.

Printable Version

Many websites have links to printable versions of pages. When you click, the URL will change, and the same page remains (but without the heavy graphics or background images). Unfortunately, this is also seen as duplicate content. It is not quite so bad because it is at least on the same domain; nevertheless, it is still problematic because Google must consider which page is the primary content page. How does it know which of the two pages should be displayed in the search results? To help with this, you should use your `robots.txt` file.

Setup and Configure a robots.txt File

A robots.txt file is a simple text file that allows you to exclude specific pages or ranges of pages from the search engines. It tells the search engines what can and cannot be crawled. RSS feeds, style sheets, javascript, and duplicate content are often prevented from crawling.

For example, many websites have a printable version that they don't want indexed by the search engines, since they could incur a duplicate content penalty. Usually the printable version is built into the template so when you click on it, the URL changes to include something like "printable" in it. The key is to identify what this is and then add it to the exclusion list of your robots.txt file.

As you add your robots.txt file entries, you can then log in to your Google Webmaster Tools account to test some of your exclusions or allows entries. For more information on robots.txt files, go to www.robotstxt.org. For a great SEO article on robots.txt, visit http://bit.ly/robotsseo.

Sneaky Things to Be Aware of

Case Sensitivity

The search engines are extremely sensitive. If you change the case of a page name from "HomePage.htm" to "homepage.htm" many search engines will see this as a completely new page with zero page rank. Ensure you take this into account when linking internally also.

Things to Avoid

- Don't use frames.
- Don't use invisible text. (The search engines see this as a high probability of spam.)

- Be careful with redirect headers. (Ensure you use permanent redirects or temporary redirects as appropriate.)
- Be careful with your robots.txt file. (Don't accidentally "`disallow *`" as this will prevent the search engines from indexing any of your site.)
- Don't create pages greater than 100KB in file size.
- Try to avoid using images where you could use text.

Emulate the Search Engines

Try using a search spider simulator such as: http://bit.ly/spideremulate You can enter your URL and it will provide a summary of what the search engines are actually seeing on your site. For example, if your site is heavy on images with text in them, you'll see that the search engines cannot crawl text that is in an image, which is why you should avoid placing text in images.

Black Hat Versus White Hat

When I first started getting involved with search engine strategies, I had built a website, www.holidayhomerental.co.uk, that had quickly grown to more than 20,000 rental properties spread throughout the United Kingdom. The number of properties resulted in more than 150,000 pages of content. Trying to get the search engines to take some or all the content was difficult at best. To try to speed things up, I attempted a number of what are now known as "black hat" techniques.

Black Hat

A simple example of this is using white text on a white background in the main website template so the same keywords appear on every single page. Although a person would not see them, the search engines would.

Every time I tried a black hat approach, it resulted in a painful lesson until I finally learned that no matter what I thought up in terms of trying to manipulate the search engines, Google had already thought of it and factored such changes into its equation, ultimately causing my website to appear in lower positions in the search results.

White Hat

Always stick with white hat approaches to search engine strategies. Unsolicited natural links from relevant keywords and regularly updated unique text are key white hat strategies. Don't be tempted to pay someone to generate a 1,000 links to your site. Google and the others will recognize this as black hat manipulation and will penalize you for it by lowering the credibility of your site in the search engines, which will adversely affect your position in the search results.

Grey Hat

Of course not everything is black or white. For example, when I was trying to find a good source of content for all the towns and counties for my UK site, I eventually decided I would syndicate content from Wikipedia. At the time, the licensing model of Wikipedia meant that you could copy content from its website onto any other website as long as you didn't alter it and you acknowledged it came from Wikipedia. Using this example, I used a program to scrap the description of thousands of locations around the UK into a local database of my own. This in itself is far from black hat because the search engines will recognize it as duplication of the Wikipedia content. However, instead of immediately posting this copied content, I left it in the database, waited for a year, and then uploaded it to the site. Wikipedia changes all the time, and the descriptions of many of the locations were different from when they were first copied. This meant the percentage of duplicate content was reduced, thus increasing my chances of these new location pages being indexed by Google and the other search engines. The downside to this approach, of course, is that much of the content was out of date, but in the interest of attracting traffic, it seemed to be worth it.

Summary

Ensure you address the most basic SEO components (titles, header tags). Then ensure you have the right tools in place to measure the performance of your SEO and your website in general. Outline a business plan that will align your social web strategy with your search engine strategy, since they go hand in hand. For example, your social web strategy may dictate that all your member- or donor-generated content should be restricted to members only, which means the search engines cannot see it. If this is the case, then displaying member's only content on the home page is not going to help with the search engines because the search engine is not a "member" and will therefore not see any of the content. When aligning both strategies, a compromise might be found whereby the association displays only the first 100 words of any member- or donor-generated content to the public (which means the search engines can see it).

Finally, SEO is not an overnight process. Often it can take up to six months for Google to acknowledge a change to your site. It may take another six months for Google to endorse it within the appropriate search engine results pages (SERPs).

CHAPTER 10

Engagement 1—Goals, Identification, and Education

This chapter will explain how establishing goals, success metrics, and timeframes are critical to successful engagement through social media. You'll learn how to identify where your most-engaged constituents are and how to challenge them. Finally, the chapter discusses the importance of educating staff, volunteer leaders, and members at large about why the social initiatives are important.

Phase 1—Identify Your Goals

Before figuring out your social strategy, you first need to know what your goals are. After all, if you do not have goals, it will be impossible to measure success. Often the first goal is obvious: "We want to get more people to our website" or "We want to improve member engagement." It is usually more involved than this, however. For example, a charitable foundation's goal might be to generate awareness, while a trade association might focus on legislative outreach (government affairs). Even when looking at a traditional professional society, the goal still may not be to improve member engagement. After all, once you start exploring and asking why and what needs to be achieved, you might find that improved engagement is just part of the path to a larger goal of improving retention. This, in turn, could be part of a larger goal to increase membership.

Engagement Path

To help demonstrate how the engagement path can help, let's assume the Widget Makers Association (WMA) has formed an in-house Social Strategy Task Force (SSTF) that is composed of a senior representative from each department and the staff liaison to the volunteer-run Technology Advisory Council (TAC). The TAC is kept apprised of the progress with regular updates and can provide feedback through the staff liaison but, because of unreasonable time constraints, does not actively sit at the table during the SSTF meetings.

After the SSTF met to discuss the goals of the social initiative, they collectively formed the following Engagement Path:

- Increase Engagement
- Improve Retention
- Grow Membership
- Expand Awareness of the Discipline

If your association chooses this exercise, ensure it is done collaboratively. It is imperative to include key stakeholders not only to achieve global buy-in and ownership for the project but also to help set realistic expectations about measurable results—what to expect and when to expect it. After you have collectively agreed on your engagement path, you should discuss how to measure and recognize success at the various milestones. This will also be useful when setting timeframes for accomplishing goals.

Example of a Success Plan

Once the SSTF has determined what the engagement path is and has confirmed the path is in alignment with the organization's mission and vision statement, it is the time to document how success will be measured and the timeframes that need to be met. Below is an example of a "success plan" that the SSTF might produce as part of the "goal identification" phase of the WMA strategic plan.

Goal Identification Phase

Increase Engagement

The only metrics the WMA has are based on the Google analytics report of the current website. For the January through June period of the previous year, the site averaged 50,000 unique visitors per month. The expectation is that the launch of the site will likely result in a sudden increase in activity (friending, community invitations, eGroup postings, blog creation) and will then drop back down to an improved but steadily increasing number.

When measuring success, the WMA will compare the six months after the social launch to the corresponding six months from the previous year. Success will be defined as a 20 percent increase in traffic recorded in the first month over the same month last year and then a gradual 5 percent to 20 percent increase over the following five months compared to the same months last year.

The new social networking engagement platform will provide much more detailed reports on specific types of member engagement, such as logins, friend requests, blogs created, ratings, comments, and other factors. Three months after the initial launch, the SSTF will review the new engagement reports provided by the social platform to help set future expectations on network growth. Ultimately success will be determined by a steady increase in traffic to the site and overall engagement generated from that traffic.

WMA will use the same Google Analytics code for the new social platform as it does for its main www website in order to more easily obtain a holistic view of overall engagement.

Improve Retention

While the first goal (to increase engagement) is more immediately measurable (within the first six months or so), improving retention is a much more distant goal.* If the WMA go-live date is January 1, 2010, it will not be possible to accurately measure retention until June 1, 2011. Even at that time, retention will not be affected, since this is essentially the result of the first day of the launch. The first six months' worth of effort will not be accurately measurable until December 2011. As an interim measure, staff will count the number of renewals that are

* It's almost impossible to immediately measure improved retention for an association like the WMA, which bills annually. For example, the usual timeframe to measure any impact on retention is 12 months from the date of the go-live date of the social platform, plus three months for the grace period, plus another two months for the reinstatement period (the period after which expired members have been dropped and during which the WMA can reinstate them as members without affecting their original join date).

processed in the six months after the January 2010 go-live date and compare to the previous year. Using this method, the results may not be accurate enough to report because of the irregularity of cancellations, late renewals, and reinstatements, but they may be used informally to try to identify any trends.

Grow Membership

The ability to grow membership can be calculated many ways. Since the first measurement of performance will be taken six months after the January 2010 go-live date, the WMA will wait until the June 30 late renewal period has ended on August 1. The SSTF will not wait until the reinstatement period is over before trying to measure, since reinstatements are minimal. On August 1, staff will run a report that will show the total number of the WMA members as of August 1, 2010, compared to August 1, 2011.

There are problems with this type of reporting, since it is not just counting new members (member growth) but also the retention period for at least six months before the go-live date. As such, staff might also report on the total number of new membership applications processed and approved during the six-month period compared with the same period the previous year.

Membership growth is also tied to retention, since growth can occur simply from improved retention, and is not only about the new membership applications received. Questions will be added to the traditional surveys for both new members and dropped members to try to determine if the new social tools had any impact on decisions to join or drop as well as to judge overall satisfaction of the new initiatives. For example:

1. Are you aware of the WMA professional social network?
2. If yes, how satisfied were you with the network tools? (Provide 1 to 5 scale for answer.)
3. If no, would you be interested in trying it for a trial period to see if it would help justify renewing your membership?
4. If yes, are there any areas that you think could be improved with this service? (Give details.)

Even though the numbers will be reviewed internally from July 2010, these numbers cannot be reported on properly until after the end of the late renewal period in August 2010. After this period, little or no change is expected in the first three months and then a very gradual increase over the following three months (between 0 percent and 2 percent). Since many of the tools require marketing to the membership and educating the members about the benefits and the concept of professional branding, the more noticeable growth (above 2 percent) likely will not start to take effect until February 2011, after the key marketing initiatives have been implemented.

Success will be realized if membership growth as a result of the professional social network has increased by 2 percent by the end of February 2011.

Expand Awareness of the Discipline

While the retention and membership growth goals are more distant, the ability to expand awareness can be measured by a number of factors. The following two barometers will be used as awareness measurement:

- Number of unique visitors to the website
- Number of new pages indexed in the search engines

Using the same reports as indicated in the "Increase Engagement" section above, emphasis should be placed on which pages are being viewed. For example, if the pages that are generating greater traffic are members-only pages, then awareness of the discipline has not necessarily been increased. However, an increase in unique visitors to public pages, such as the "About Us" section or "Member Benefits" section, is a strong indication that awareness of the discipline has been expanded.

The number of new pages indexed by the search engines can be measured because the new social platform will have its own domain name (i.e., community.wma.org), which is different from the regular website, which is www.wma.org. This makes it easy to measure, since before the website goes live, there will be zero pages in the search indexes that begin with community.wma.org. After six months, we can simply search for site:community.wma.org, and get the total number of pages indexed by Google, Yahoo, Bing, and others.

The above two measurements are leading indicators of success in this area. A 7 percent increase in traffic to the top five most likely visited (public) pages by people who are new to the discipline would be considered successful.

Success within the community section will be measured by the number of indexed pages in the search engines. The more pages that are open to the public, the more pages will be indexed and the greater the exposure of the discipline.

Conclusion of Phase 1—Identify Your Goals

The importance of Phase 1 cannot be understated. The examples above clearly show that success is not what many might believe, such as "Ten percent of our membership will start a blog in the first three months," or "A third of the membership will actively post messages to the listserver." Creating something similar to an SSTF not only gives everyone a say in the goals but also sets realistic expectations about measurable outcomes. Having buy-in for a project of this magnitude, which really does affect every area of the organization, is critical to the overall success—because everyone must understand what success really is.

Phase 2—Educating the Stakeholders

The first part of this phase should be to determine who your stakeholders are and what their level of influence/importance is over the project and its success. The typical stakeholders of an association are the staff, volunteer leadership, and members; there may be others, but this is a good place to start.

Once the stakeholders have been identified, the mission is then to educate them about how to "think social." This is easier said than done, as it first requires a solid understanding of the social web, and examples are required to get them started. The social web is full of creative and innovative tools and features. Stakeholders should be trained to think creatively, so innovation will flourish. For example, when brainstorming ideas, someone from the conference department might consider opening up all the conference event submissions for the members to vote on instead of using the traditional committee to select the sessions. When brainstorming ideas about how different departments might leverage social engagement, ensure that every idea is perceived to be appreciated, as this will encourage more out-of-the-box thinking by stakeholders.

When training the stakeholders, the goal of the exercise depends on the stakeholder in question. The following are some sample ideas that matured into action items to implement. This training exercise will not just generate some very interesting ideas but also will help gain that all important buy-in, especially when some of the stakeholder ideas actually materialize and are credited accordingly.

Staff

Every department needs to understand why the social web is important to their areas. To help staff with this exercise, after teaching them the fundamentals of the social web, split the participants into brainstorming groups. Do not split them into departments; ensure they are cross-pollinated because often some of the best ideas are generated from people who do not have the usual assumptions and are not too close to the forest to see the trees.

Assign each group a different functional area such as education, meetings, or membership, and then ask the department staffer to explain what their department does and how it typically operates. While doing so, try to encourage the rest of the group to challenge the assumptions and start coming up with ideas about how the social aspects of the web might be integrated.

The list of ideas generated may be endless, but often the results are similar from association to association. For example, the Medical Group Management Association (MGMA) generated the following ideas for their meetings and events area:

Functional Department: Meetings and Events

The events department will be open to any ideas that can help promote their conference, workshops, webinars, or symposiums as well as enhance the value of the events to prospective exhibitors. The social web offers numerous opportunities to do all of the above. Specifically:

Friend Attendees

When people log in to the meeting community website, show them which people they have friended are attending. If the person is not logged in, show a dynamic control displaying the most recent registrants with a link to see who else is registering and linking to their professional profiles. If your association is too conservative to display a list of people, consider showing a list of company names from which the registrants are coming. This helps fulfill the purpose without revealing personal identities. Using a similar approach, you should show either the job titles or functional job titles of the attendees to help demonstrate the level of the event. This is especially true when there are a lot of C-level attendees.

Registration

When someone registers, after clicking on the submit button on the payment page, instead of sending them to a "thank you" page, send them to a referral page where they are asked to invite five of their friends to attend the meeting. This example tends to resonate well with the events staff because most organizations suffer from being too dependent on email. If you can, diversify from generic blast emails to the membership at large who have not yet registered. Logically, having a member invite another member to an event, will be perceived differently than the traditional blast email from the association, hopefully resulting in a better response rate.

Exhibitor/Vendor Directory/Buyer's Guide

When the American Wind Energy Association (AWEA) discussed the idea of a buyer's guide, the conversation started with the existing buyer's guide, and it led to the idea of allowing members to rate and review the company profiles. This is a sensitive area. After all, companies normally pay to be in the guide. There is fear of lost revenue if a member rates a company or product negatively, so a company may want its profile removed from the directory. This is a valid concern, but there are a number of ways around it. For example, the entire business model of the buyer's guide could be changed so every company is listed for free (whether they want to be or not), but only those companies that pay receive premium placement and/or have the ability to post a rebuttal to any member comment submitted. Another option is to allow paid listings to approve or decline reviews. Of course, the latter option reduces the transparency and authenticity that the social web is supposed to produce; nevertheless, similar to the "delete" option when moderating blogs, it is an option.

The buyer's guide has close ties to the exhibitor directory, and similar ideas were discussed in this area. Of course, the stakes can be much greater, since you don't want to run the risk of losing an exhibitor.

For those organizations that do not have a buyer's guide, vendor directory, or anything like this, ask your social platform provider if you can create a company directory that pulls company profiles out of your Association Management System (AMS) based on a specific member type or set of member types. Usually the AMS also captures individuals that are attached to any specific company as well, so this should be fairly easy to manage from the AMS itself.

Functional Department: Membership

The Society of Naval Architecture and Marine Engineering (SNAME) conducted a workshop called "Think Social" where all departments were challenged to come up with ideas on how to leverage the social web. While they discussed all their functional areas, some great ideas emerged. Using the membership department, here are a few examples:

Mentoring

Encourage members to take part in a mentoring program by becoming mentors or mentees. This would work like Facebook, allowing you to install applications and then "throw" them at your friends. Participants would use the same referral control that the Medical Group Management Association developed for event registration to invite friends to become a mentor or a mentee. After users install the mentoring application in their professional profiles, they will be taken to a dynamic list of possible matches based on their own demographics. Each category will then link to the social network (member directory) list of search results. To see an example of how this works, visit: http://bit.ly/mentorreferral.

Get-a-Member Campaign

Usually when brainstorming ways to implement social media, someone will come up with a "Get a Member" campaign idea. The way you implement such a campaign really depends on your audience. For example, if you have a relatively low market penetration due to lack of association exposure, then it might be worthwhile trying to leverage the public outposts to generate nonmember exposure.

You can create a custom application within Facebook that allows anyone to "Refer a Friend" to your nonprofit. The application can be quite simple, such as asking the users if they are interested in accepting free trial membership in the organization. If so, they are prompted to enter their name and email address. Once they click on submit, they are asked to invite their friends into the trial membership as well. One idea to incentivize this viral part of the application is to associate the length of the trial membership with the number of invites they send out to their friends list. Building Facebook applications is outside the scope of this book, but one thing to be aware of is that Facebook will not give you any information about who someone is, just demographic information about them. The only way any application can know who users are is if the application specifically asks for the information (such as name and email) and users enter it. To see an example of a prototype Facebook viral app I created for associations using the Facebook Mark-Up Language, see http://bit.ly/AreYouPaidEnough.

If the association already has a deep market penetration and knows most of the prospective members are already in their database as nonmembers, then create a viral application within your own website that invites members to take part in the member-get-a-member campaign. The difference is that the campaign is run virally so members invite other members to refer their non-member peers. Every referral is tracked using tracking codes. Similar to having a "snowball fight" in Facebook, it is actually possible to have a winner of this type of viral application pyramid. Winners should obviously be rewarded in some way.

Functional Department: Creative Services/Publishing

The Risk & Insurance Management Society, Inc. (RIMS), Creative Department was discussing innovative ways they could take their printed magazine to the next level. The general idea was to reinvent the online version of the magazine so it would not just reproduce the same articles as in the print version but would become a publication that would allow far greater interaction with the end users. A number of ideas came to light but some highlights included:

Short URLs Linking to the Corresponding Online Article

Members will have the ability to rate and review as well as blog and discuss. While this idea has not been implemented yet, I believe it will be implemented. The idea was to cross-promote both the printed and online platforms. For example, the idea of placing a shortcut "Go URL" next to every printed article such as:

> Rate/Review/Share/Forward/Print: http://www.snama.org/020414

The numbers at the end of the URL correspond to the volume number, issue number, and article number. When readers type in this short URL, the system not only tracks who used the URL and when, but also takes them directly to the page that will allow them to engage by forwarding to a friend, rating, reviewing, or taking part in any of the other social media options.

Flexible Permissions

This idea is not directly tied to the social web except that it does help fulfill the mission of expanding the knowledge of the association's discipline while providing new member benefits. The idea here was to restrict the association's online magazine to members only. This idea is not new. What is new is the ability to then open the permissions for any issue or article after a period of time. When the group examined what the member benefits of the magazine were, the answer always came down to the valuable content of the articles in the magazine. It was then acknowledged that the value diminished over a period of time. As a result, they modified the magazine publishing system (MPS) to be a members-only benefit for the first 30 days, but after this time, each issue would be available to the public and, most importantly, to the search engines. This means thousands of articles in the archive would be exposed to the public, causing an exponential growth in search engine-generated traffic after a period of time. However, the true member benefit has been retained, since only members can access the most recent edition.

Wiki Glossary

The original idea of the purpose-built glossary came from RIMS. Like many associations, RIMS had a paper glossary of terms, phrases, and acronyms for the industry that was printed many years earlier and had not been updated. The idea was to turn the glossary into an online wiki and ask the members to help update it. The wiki glossary embraces all the principles of the social web by allowing ratings, comments, related URLs, and, most importantly from a wiki perspective, accountability, as members have their names and photos displayed next to their edited version of the entry.

Social Web Education

Educating staff will be worthwhile not just in generating buy-in and ownership but also in developing a tremendous list of ideas and action items that can be easily implemented. The challenge with all these ideas is to prioritize them. When doing so, involve the vendor of your social platform or a consultant who can quickly assess the difficulty. You may be surprised that many of the items (such as the magazine system or the company directory) will be workable from an out-of-the-box solution with little to no effort. The vendor should at least be able to give an indication whether any specific item is a large-, medium-, or small-scale project, which will help with prioritization.

Volunteer Leadership

The education of your volunteer leadership and the members at large will be similar to educating your staff. The volunteer leaders must understand why the social web is important for the organization as well as why it is important to them. The leaders will typically be the ones coming up with ideas and asking questions to which the regular members also will want the answers. These leaders will most likely be the champions of various industry or interest segments, too.

Personal URLs (PURLs)

While in the education phase of the social web with the leadership of Infocomm International (an organization that represents the audio visual industry), one board member mentioned that he often received emails from peers with their LinkedIn profile as part of the email signature. A discussion ensued about why LinkedIn was representing those professionals instead of Infocomm, which was the representative body for the A/V industry. If members are going to promote their professional profile, why not give them a simple Infocomm URL for this purpose? This idea was explored further and has been adopted by many associations as part of their social strategy. Most associations that have done this also provide demographic reports to the members that tell them how many times their PURL has been used. In some instances, the association might reward the member who has generated the most exposure to their profile through their PURL. The association would ask members to add the PURL to their email signature like so:

View My Professional Profile: www.SNAMA.org/AndySteggles

Another example can be seen at: www.nysaenet.org/AndySteggles

Social Web Expectations

Leaders should have clear expectations of the social web. It is imperative that the leadership fully understands and buys into the goals of the initiative, how they align with the organization's mission and vision, and how success will be measured and over what timeframe. When demonstrating success metrics, show leaders sample reports that they can expect to see at the end of the milestone periods. Most of these are easily generated. Introduce them to the concept of engagement points and the ability to measure not just online engagement but overall engagement in a way that has never been possible before. (See Chapter 11 on engagement and recognition.) It is an excellent opportunity to make them understand how the association is really pushing itself and is on the cutting edge of membership engagement techniques.

Members at Large

There is much overlap with the education of the volunteer leadership and members at large. The main difference is that by the time you get to educating the members, the platform should be fully tested and launched. Usually, helping members understand the benefits of the social initiative will be part of your overall marketing plan for the social platform. Typically, it will involve a series of webinars that can be recorded and reused as needed, such as "Top three things you need to know about your industry social network." Annual conferences also present great opportunities to educate members. Consider having someone at your booth performing a demonstration of the platform or have an educational session on career development that dedicates a segment to the new program.

Professional Branding

One of the most important things to educate your members about is the concept of their professional brand. Ask your members if they have ever searched for their own name in Google. Almost everyone has. Ask them what they would like to see as the number-one result. Is it a Speedo photo in Facebook, a professional profile in LinkedIn, or an industry profile from your organization's website? Facebook is not normally the top choice for most seasoned professionals. But why choose the association profile over the LinkedIn profile? The answer is that the association represents their industry and has much more relevant information about them, such as education events attended, volunteer activities within the association, blogs and discussion group postings, wiki entries edited, and so forth. The association profile is really a living profile that reflects behavioral data versus a Linkedin or Facebook profile that relies on declared data. For example, if you attend an event, you're automatically added to the respective event community and the event is automatically added to your professional association's profile, but on the other sites, you'd have to manually enter information about your event attendance.

This is an ideal opportunity to remind members that they are responsible for monitoring their own brand. They should have Google alerts set up for their own name and possibly their organization's name so they are alerted the moment Google discovers any new information on the web that mentions them. While the association can help members establish their professional brands, the members themselves need to take ownership of their overall search engine exposure.

Privacy Concerns

There will always be some members who do not want anything displayed about them at all. They need the assurance that they are in charge of their own profiles and they decide which permissions they wish to assign. The usual permission options for elements of profiles are classified along the lines of:

- Public: Anyone, including the search engines
- Authenticated: Anyone who is logged in, including nonmembers
- Members: Only members
- Friends: Only those people with whom I have established a trust relationship

As the association, you get to set the defaults, but a member may override them. Perhaps they want their email address displayed to any member instead of the association default that may have been to display email address only to "friends." Every possible element of the member profile is broken down into the smallest detail to give members control over what can and cannot be seen and by whom. This is an important point to emphasize to all members.

Identify Existing Engaged Members/Donors

As you approach launch day, you should already have an outline of a marketing plan. While the marketing plan should help generate awareness of this new member benefit, the best way to generate awareness is for engaged members to provide valuable content.

Generating engagement is easier said than done. Before heading on a quest to get members to blog, edit wikis, or post questions on the forums, consider approaching members who are already engaged in a more traditional capacity. Who are the currently engaged members of your nonprofit? For example, you may have chapter officers or committee members. What is the likelihood that they will create some content if you ask them to perform some kind of very specific task such as "find two phrases in the glossary and update them," "create a blog about your experience serving on the membership committee," or "think of a provocative industry-specific question and submit it to the eGroups." If a random member with an average level of engagement receives a request to "please post an entry on our new blogging platform," the odds are it will be ignored. Compare this to the success rate of going the extra step and asking the membership committee member or the New York Chapter VP of Finance to do something similar, and you will likely see a significant improvement in response rate.

The best motivator to get people engaged is when they see how other people are recognized for their contributions. Challenge your already engaged members and then approach other members with average levels of engagement.

Examples of Engagement Categories

Here are some examples of where you can find already engaged members (and nonmembers if you want to include them):

- Current committee members
- Past committee members
- Current chapter officers
- Past chapter officers
- Speakers (at your upcoming annual conference)
- Speakers (at your previous conferences/events)

- Authors (for your print magazine or online newsletters)
- Session suggestion submitters (for your annual conference)
- Session suggestion submitters (for previous conferences/events)
- eGroup posters (people who have posted a question to the eGroups/listservers)
- eGroup replies (people who have posted a reply to the eGroups/listservers)
- Award recipients

It should not be difficult to identify hundreds of already engaged members and nonmembers. Of course, what initially looked like a fairly straightforward proposition is now turning into a much more involved process due to the sheer volume of categories. To help get around this dilemma, it is possible to automate the process. Assign a weight to the categories above. The weighting is supposed to dictate the likelihood of the person's responding to the request for engagement. Once this is assigned, your IT staff will need to run a number of queries to identify all the people that match any of the criteria and put them into an engagement table.

Example of an Engagement Category Table

Engagement Category	Probability of Engagement (100 = high likelyhood, 0=low likelyhood)
2009 magazine author	90
Failed magazine author	80
Speaker	85
Exhibitor	50
Chapter officer	80
Committee member	85
Donor	70
Nonmember	10
2006 abstract submitter	55
Member	40

Weighting the various categories is subjective. After all, who is to say that a speaker is more likely to be engaged than an exhibitor? The only real way to find out is by emailing both and testing. This doesn't need to be an exact science however, so the values can be adjusted as you start to view the results.

Without going into too much technical detail, the goal is to end up with every possible match to the above with the highest level of engagement weighting. For example, if I have submitted a session suggestion for a previous conference but have also submitted one for the upcoming conference, the latter would be weighted more highly in terms of likelihood of getting a response to generate engagement. In this example, if I qualified for both criteria, only the highest level of engagement will be recorded in the database. Alternatively, you can record every piece of engagement for all individuals in the engagement table but pull only the highest level when you actually generate the email to the individual.

So the next step in this exercise is to create a personalized, carefully written email based on the category of the engagement level. For example, for a past committee member, the email might be something along the lines of:

Sample of Targeted Engagement Request Email: Past Committee Member

> [Firstname],
>
> I'm writing to you because you are a former committee member of WMA and a known leader in our industry. I hope you can help us with the launch of our new professional network for WMA members. Specifically, if you could spare approximately 20 minutes, would you pick an industry-specific topic and write a couple of paragraphs giving your thoughts and opinions about the topic? You choose the topic. All we ask is that it is relevant to the membership at large. To participate, please click on the link below, and log in with your email address and password and then submit your posting.
>
> In return for your time, we will be recognizing you and several others who participate by displaying an excerpt with a link to your posting on the new community home page. Since this will be your first WMA posting of this nature, we will also add a digital ribbon to your profile as a way of recognizing your contribution.
>
> Please let me know if you're willing to help us with the launch of this network.
>
> Thank you in advance,
>
> Andy Steggles
> WMA

The key is the partial personalization of the message that is crafted to play on different areas of emotion (ego being a simple one) of the user. Notice how I have not used the word "blog" and instead simply asked them to submit their opinion/thoughts? Also notice how I have tried to incentivize them by offering recognition on both the community home page as well as their individual profile. The wording and the rewards would be adjusted to reflect the culture of both your industry and its members.

Anti-Spam

Note that "Dear" was not added before the first name. Adding "Dear" not only triggers spam filters but also immediately alerts the recipient that the message is likely to be a spam or marketing message. How often do you send a regular email to someone and start it with "Dear"? Also avoid adding anything related to "free," "competition," or "win" as incentives, as they are all common spam flags.

Randomness of Emails and a Word of Warning

Once you have written all the emails, you then need to send them randomly, generating a few emails to the various members on a scheduled basis. The number and frequency will be different for every association and can be calculated by testing. Perhaps try 100 emails a day for three days in a row, and then measure the response to determine if this is too much or too little, adjusting accordingly.

When I originally took this approach, I did not randomize the emails, so they were generated based on the different categories. As a result, in the first week, more than 40 speakers created blogs about their upcoming sessions at the annual conference. Obviously, the lack of diversity in the blogs didn't bode well with the casual web surfers which were reading them. Lesson learned.

Summary

Engagement strategy is a multistep process. This chapter has covered some of the critical elements. The importance of success metrics, goals, and timeframes has been emphasized as well as the importance of educating the key stakeholders and challenging already engaged members to participate in this new medium. Before proceeding with this step, be sure to outline your blogging and other engagement strategies, as discussed in upcoming chapters.

CHAPTER 11

Engagement 2—Measure, Recognize, and Reward

A successful social strategy will lead to improved engagement. According to ASAE & The Center's *The Decision to Volunteer* (August 2008) http://bit.ly/decisionto, improved engagement will have a direct, positive correlation to improved retention. How can an organization measure, recognize, and reward its members' or donors' engagement?

Return on Engagement (ROE)

In many ways, 2008 was the year of social media and 2009 was the year of social media engagement. According to Lehman Associates, 31 percent of associations are either integrating social initiatives or budgeting to do so, Association Trends Supplement, June 2008 (http://bit.ly/lehmansocmed). So let's assume you've decided to push ahead with your social initiative, how can you promote its use, generate revenue, increase efficiency, and most importantly, measure the results? How can you encourage your members to become engaged online?

Let's assume you are a small association, and you decide to invest $1,000 to upgrade your online member directory to a full-fledged private social platform. Traditionally, you may have looked for a return on investment (ROI) for that $1,000, perhaps by measuring the amount of banner revenue from the increased traffic to your site.

Instead of focusing on ROI, start looking for a return on engagement (ROE) which is more easily measured. The $1,000 investment may provide a platform, but with the right engagement strategy, members will perform activities that provide more value for their peers as well as personal brand recognition for themselves. The return on engagement (ROE) is the amount of activity and what results from it, such as improved retention and member growth. While it takes a while to detect a change in your membership retention rate, you can immediately see the member engagement rate (MER). MER is optionally a barometer for measuring success.

Usually online survey campaigns might generate most responses within the first 48 hours of sending the link. The same is often true of an engagement campaign. For example, if you create a campaign for your upcoming conference speakers, asking them to blog about their sessions, within 48 hours you will likely have a pretty good idea of the success of that campaign.

In many ways, ROE is similar to measuring traditional marketing metrics, except you are not sending a postcard and seeing how many registrations you receive or new members join. Instead, you are asking members to blog, edit a wiki, befriend colleagues, and/or share files (you may not use those words of course, but functionally that is what you want them to do). You are asking your members to create their own brands within their industry, raise their profiles, educate peers, and establish their online professional resumes as social profiles.

Member Engagement Rate (MER)

What is the member engagement rate? You need only a 1 percent success rate to generate valuable content for the majority of the membership. You can continue to measure the success of that one campaign forever. While 10 percent of the speakers may have created a blog entry within 48 hours, how many will return to create another blog a couple of weeks later and ultimately become regular bloggers? All engagement can be represented by points and therefore quantified and used to benchmark the results. The more engagement activities your members perform, the higher the MER.

Online Engagement

Associations and nonprofits have long struggled to keep their members active. With the help of more traditional component-based structures such as geographically-based chapters, special interest or industry groups, donation campaigns, legislative calls to action, professional development initiatives, and attendance at the annual conference, associations have offered a broad array of opportunities for members to be engaged in the offline (in-person) world. But what about the new online world?

The social web offers a whole new assortment of engagement opportunities with tremendous potential. To measure engagement, you first must identify the functional areas of your social platform to determine which are measurable from a technical perspective. Once these areas have been identified, the measurable engagement activities can also be identified.

The functional areas include, but are not limited to, blogs, wikis, discussion groups, the member/donor directory (social network), and sharing (any type of files). The engagement opportunities associated with these activities are numerous. Here are some of these functional areas and their respective engagement activities:

Blog Engagement Activities

Read	Add Author as Friend/Contact
Create	Print
Rate	Subscribe to RSS Feed
Comment	Trackback
Rate a Comment	Forward to a friend
Add Related Link	Add to Favorites
Rate Related Link	

Discussion Group Engagement Activities

Read	Add Author as Friend/Contact
Create	Print
Rate	Subscribe to RSS Feed
Reply to Sender	View Thread
Reply to Discussion Group	Forward to a friend
Add Related Link	Add to Favorites
Rate Related Link	Attach/Share a File

Profile/Directory Activities

Upload Photo	Set Privacy Preferences
Add Bio	Add Member as a Friend/Contact
Select Interests	Rate Contacts
Update Demographics	Add Certifications/Designations
Add Employment History	Create a Community
Add Education Details	Join a Community
Search Directory	Invite Contact to Join a Community

Similar engagement opportunities may exist in your wiki and sharing environments or in other functional areas such as your job bank or buyer's guide. Platform selection is of paramount importance when it comes to measuring engagement. (See Chapter 16 on how to choose a social platform.) After all, if you can't record the activity, you can't measure it.

An association Resource Library also offers new opportunities, such as the ability to share a file, upload a video, or download a podcast. With the right technology, this activity can easily be tracked and measured as every "share" would contain a tracking ID that will tell you how many times that share has been forwarded or used.

When reading a blog, you may not wish to comment but, instead, create a blog response to a posting. Discuss the posting via a discussion group, or even create a wiki entry based on a blog. The key to engagement is to make things as easy as possible, so when someone is reading a blog entry and sees "Discuss This" and "Blog This," little or no effort is involved in performing these actions.

Measuring Engagement

Engagement Center

Engagement opportunities have limited usefulness without the ability to measure and reward. Assuming your selected social platform is able to track all the available activities associated with these new social technologies, you have the opportunity to tie them into your mission and vision statement.

For example, let's say that the mission of the American Automobile Association might be to promote safer roads. With such a broad mission, one key area of opportunity would be to flood the search engines with content that supports this mission. In this instance, blog creation would be high on your social strategy agenda. A comprehensive engagement center allows you to view your social engagement activities and assign point values to each. Points are a useful way of measuring engagement, allowing you to identify and reward the people with the most points (those who are most engaged).

If you could assign a point value from 0 to 10 to each of the engagement activities listed earlier for blogging, what values would you assign? Of course, you should not just assign points arbitrarily; the decisions need to support your overall social strategy, which, in turn, should support your vision and mission. If you have a heavy focus on peer review, then perhaps you might assign higher point values for rating journal entries than for creating new blogs. The great thing about having an effective engagement center is the ability to choose what is right for your organization. The process of assigning points is a good opportunity to generate input and interest from other senior staff and the volunteer leadership within your organization. Here are some example point values:

Blog Engagement Activities

Activity	Point Value	Activity	Point Value
Read	1	Add Author as Friend/Contact	2
Create	7	Print	1
Rate	2	Subscribe to RSS Feed	2
Comment	4	Trackback	1
Rate a Comment	1	Forward to a friend	5
Add Related Link	2	Add to Favorites	2
Rate Related Link	1		

Notice that the "Forward to a friend" activity has been assigned an unusually high point value because each instance of this activity may generate a new prospect, since the email address to which it is being forwarded is recorded.

You might be surprised that a point has been assigned for reading a blog. Keep in mind this is the most popular of all online activities and is still engagement, albeit the lowest (lurker) level.

Point Variables

Once you've assigned all the points, you may want to add a skew factor to account for positive or negative ratings. If I assign 8 points for creating a new blog entry, but that blog is then rated poorly, I might deduct points or even assign a negative value. For example, let's say I assign 7 points for creating a blog, and then I receive 3 or more negative ratings. I might then assign -10 points which would net the member a -2 overall point value for this entry, essentially penalizing the member for wasting other members' time. Obviously, you do not have to go into this much detail if you do not want to do so. Whether you actually display the point values to the member is a strategic decision. I've seen many associations switch them off so members can not see them, since they can generate too many questions. Other associations have embraced them and display the points wherever possible. Whether you display the points or not, really depends on the culture of the organization.

Similarly, if you assigned 5 points for editing a wiki entry, then you may want to skew the points based on the character count difference before and after the edit. In other words, if there were 100 characters of text in the wiki prior to the edit and now there are 300 characters, it is a reasonable assumption to say the edit was substantial. With this in mind, you may want to increase the point value based on the amount of the edit. Of course this does not take into account quality (ratings), but it is still an attribute to be considered. No system is foolproof, but the aggregated values should somehow reflect a user's overall engagement.

What to Do with the Points

So now that you have been through all the functional areas of your social platform and assigned points in a way that makes sense for your organization, what do you do with them? It ties into your overall social strategy. In a snapshot, you can see the total point value index for your entire site as well as other key information.

Example Engagement Report Used By an Association: Total Statistics Since Inception

To see more detailed examples of engagement reports, visit: http://bit.ly/engagementreport

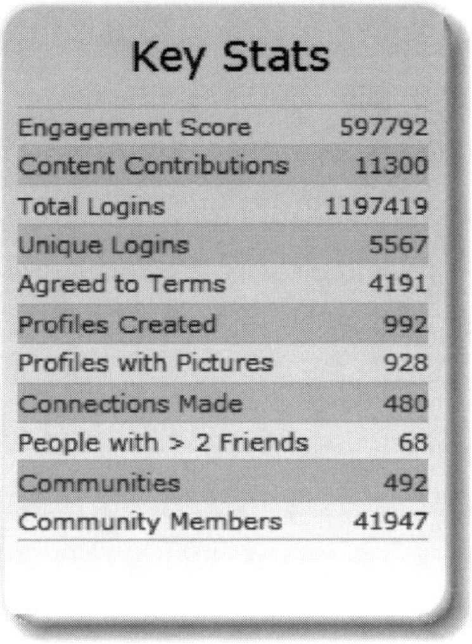

Key Stats	
Engagement Score	597792
Content Contributions	11300
Total Logins	1197419
Unique Logins	5567
Agreed to Terms	4191
Profiles Created	992
Profiles with Pictures	928
Connections Made	480
People with > 2 Friends	68
Communities	492
Community Members	41947

Most Valuable Member (MVM)

Let's move forward six months after the initial launch of your platform; this is where things get really interesting. With a click of a button, you can now answer the question, "Who is our most valuable member?" and know the associated point value. For example, the following shows a one week report for the "Most Engaged Members" of www.SNAMA.org.

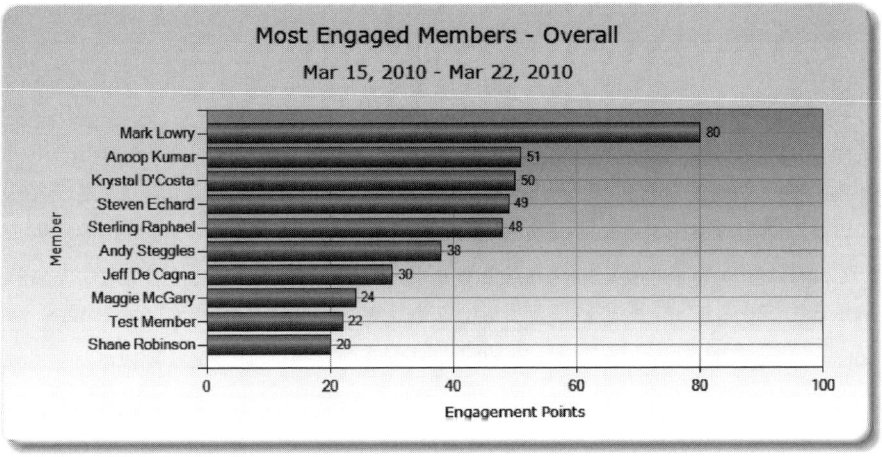

The really interesting thing about reports similar to the one above, is that when reviewing with various boards of directors, in almost every instance at least half of the people displayed as the most valuable members have not been recognized by anyone on the board! This emphasizes the fact that the social web is attracting a new type of member, one who may not be engaged using traditional media but one who is engaged using online social media.

The association may decide to award MVM status to any member with more than 200 points. If you are an MVM, when other users view your profile, they will see a nicely created digital plaque or ribbon next to your photo giving recognition.

A word of caution though: While most members have been very engaged to achieve this status, they should not be allowed to suddenly become disengaged for an extended period of time and keep the status. Indeed, if they have not generated at least X number of points within Y period of time, then they may need to start losing points. A key part of your engagement strategy is to create ongoing engagement, not just one-time engagement. Typically, you would promote the points system by letting members know their online engagement is being measured. In most cases, you would not want to declare the algorithm for generating points as this could encourage point manipulation.

Recognizing and Nurturing Thought Leaders

In social spaces, one must remember that the interaction is not just about you, like it is with email or other one-way communications. Everyone on a social network has a group or network of friends and followers. Some of them have invested considerable time and effort building large and diverse networks and are deemed "influencers" or "thought leaders" because their opinions and thoughts are respected by others within their networks. By identifying and engaging these individuals, you can extend your reach far beyond your core network—in essence, these thought leaders act as your megaphone. The following are ways you can recognize and nurture these thought leaders to reward them for their participation.

1. Provide a thought leader spotlight on your website.
2. Recognize thought leader contributions in your e-newsletter or print member publications.
3. Grant them special access to customer service or senior staff.
4. Give them discounts on publications, memberships, or meeting registration.
5. Create special badges or banners for them to add to their own websites/profiles.
6. Provide them with opportunities to promote their expertise or business.

7. Send them a special thank you premium.

Community managers must master innovative ideas to engage their constituents. Unlike chapter management, community management needs to focus more on delegating tasks to the network and less time on doing the tasks themselves. Community members need to feel a sense of ownership and achievement that will in turn help build an emotional bond with the network and further encourage engagement. Community managers must be innovative in nature, coming up with ideas to keep participants participating and expanding the social network for special projects and objectives. This next generation of managers also needs to understand how to generate media attention the PR 2.0 way. A core part of engagement is the ability to recognize and reward.

Recognize and Reward Activities

Digital Ribbons

When deciding how to recognize members, try to consider what is most valuable to your members and which levels of engagement you wish to recognize. One example that tends to resonate well with nonprofits is the concept of digital ribbons. Many associations have annual conferences where they use badge ribbons to recognize members for different types of engagement, such as chapter officer, committee member, and award recipient. Because the event may last only a few days, members can become proud of their accumulation of ribbons. This is not surprising because many have dedicated a lot of personal time to be engaged with the organization and this is often the only recognition from their peers. Even if you decide not to integrate a private social platform, consider adding a nice graphic of a ribbon next to the appropriate members in your current online member directory. It's very simple to do and is an instant win-win.

Example of an online profile with digital ribbons: http://bit.ly/andysteggles

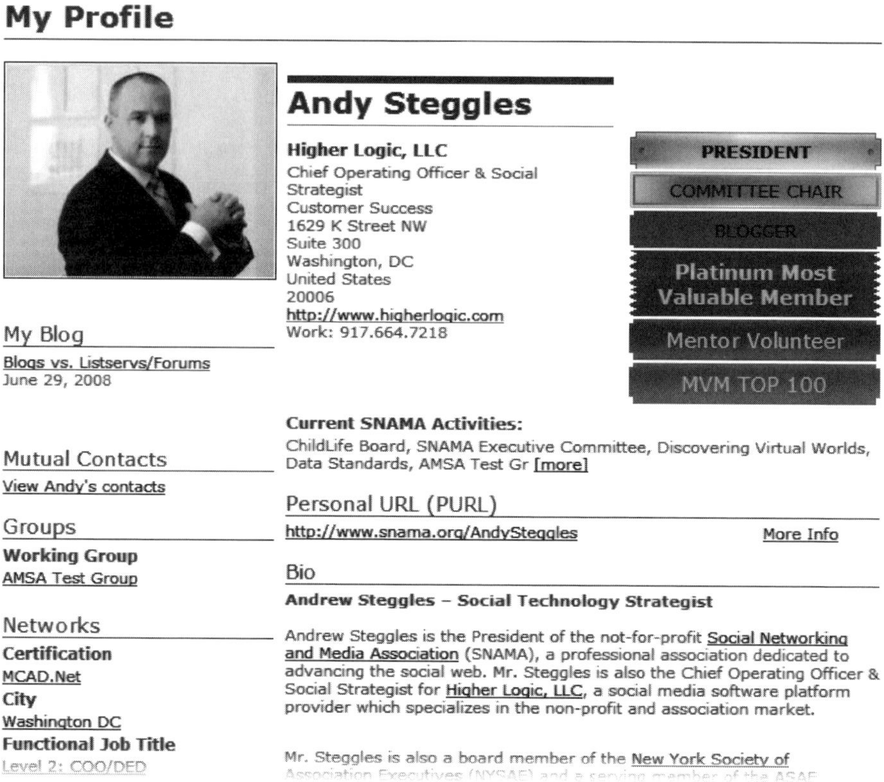

Social Badging

Social badging is a concept similar to digital ribbons. The difference is in the look as well as the purpose. For example, while you might recognize a committee member with a ribbon saying "Membership Committee," you might recognize someone who has reached "Most Valuable Member" status with a graphic image of a plaque or badge. Social badging is popular with nonprofits as a way of recognizing donations or contributions. Ribbons recognize professional activities, while badges can indicate less formal support or donation-based activities.

Digital Ribbon Types

If you decide to integrate a social platform and are interested in digital ribbons or social badges, here are some things to consider:

Community-Based Recognition

Ensure you do not have to assign ribbons individually to every eligible person. This would become a maintenance nightmare, especially when recognizing committee members and similar contributors. An effective way around this is to have the ability to assign a ribbon to a community and then if anyone is a member of a community, they will automatically have the community ribbon displayed on their profile. Keep in mind that communities can be committees, chapters, special interest groups, donors, event registrants/attendees, and so on. Community-based ribbons provide much more scalability.

Activity-Based Recognition

While most recognition may focus on communities, start thinking about what else you might want to recognize people for in a Web 2.0 world. Activity-based recognition is a way of assigning a ribbon or badge based on various actions or collections of activities. For example, if someone has joined the association within the past 6 months, they may receive a "New Member" ribbon; if I have blogged for the first time within the last six months, then I might automatically receive the "New Blogger" ribbon. Six months and one day after I have posted my first blog, I no longer qualify for the "New Blogger" ribbon and so it disappears. Instead, I qualify for the "Blogger" ribbon, which now appears in its place. Using the "skewing" variables that have been mentioned above, you might consider modifying this activity-based ribbon to remove any blogger ribbon if the member has not blogged within a given period of time.

It would be fairly simple to create an activity-based ribbon for point ranges such as everyone who scores between 200 and 400 engagement points within a given period of time. This might qualify them for a bronze-colored "Most Valuable Member." Of course, you can create as many of these as you wish. There could be bronze, silver, gold, and platinum levels. While it may not be too difficult to reach the bronze status, the silver and gold might take considerable effort. Since the more engaged members are providing such tremendous value for the rest of the association, you might consider offering a free or discounted membership renewal as a monetary reward. Of course, a lapel pin might be perceived just as valuable and may also be less expensive and equally effective.

Ad Hoc Based Ribbons

The final type of ribbon is an ad hoc ribbon for anything that does not fall under either of the above two categories. For example, you might have "Member of the Year," which might be a single member, once per year. In this instance, you would just look up an individual and assign them a ribbon. This wouldn't really be considered an activity and most likely wouldn't be a community, although you could create a community for the "Members of the Year" if you wanted.

Other Considerations of Digital Recognition

Ribbon Weighting

The first time I launched digital ribbons in a member directory, I received instant feedback: Why is Ribbon X above Ribbon Y? The "Chapter Officer" ribbon appeared above the "President" ribbon. While this might not sound important, it did highlight something I had overlooked—the ability to weight ribbons. Ensure your platform supports the ability to weight-order the ribbons.

Ribbon Component Strategy

Components are another key consideration of digital recognition. Once chapter officers start seeing ribbons and other digital bling on their member profiles, it is only a matter of time before you start receiving requests to allow the local chapter officers to add ribbons to some of their specific members. The assumption here is that the chapters are using a centralized content management system and member database, they build and manage their website using tools that you've provided. If you are using such a system, then you will know that the same social network/ member directory which is available on the main association's site is also available on the chapter site, including the display of digital ribbons.

Component ribbons may sound fairly straightforward, but consider what happens when a chapter officer assigns a "Member of the Year" ribbon to Heather McGraw. Then another member views Heather's profile on the main association's website. The implication is that the "Member of the Year" ribbon is from the main association as opposed to the chapter. To get around this issue, ensure the platform you use will allow you to specify if components are allowed to have ribbons displayed globally (on all the websites) or locally (just on the respective component website where they were originally assigned).

Fusion of Traditional and Online Recognition

For many, a digital ribbon or an MVM plaque next to their profile will suffice, while those with a significantly higher level of engagement may be further rewarded by a profile in your industry magazine or journal. Each month you could feature your top three most valuable members in a page of your printed publication. Similar to the way ASAE features a "day in the life" of a member and/or features industry blogs, you could feature/highlight your most engaged members.

Another option is feature people who have recently broken into a new level of engagement such as the silver or platinum levels which correspond to X amount of engagement points. For example, at what level might you give away the prestigious lapel pin which recognizes industry contributions?

Think of other more typical ways in which you can recognize and thank members: Perhaps present a certificate to the different members at your annual conference or have a new award for the year's most valuable member. Roy Snell, the Executive Director from the Corporate Compliance Association, recently introduced CE credits for blogs that meet specific criteria.

Think about the possibilities of such measuring techniques and how you could use the results to recognize and reward members.

Why Just Online Engagement?

The focus of this book is about online engagement surrounding your social platform. It doesn't have to stop there, however. If your platform supports it, consider assigning point values to offline engagement, too. For example, perhaps you want to reward people who:

- Renew/join
- Attend your annual conference
- Volunteer as an officer of one of your chapters
- Serve on a task force
- Author an article for your magazine
- Attend a legislative event
- Buy a book

All of the above are traditional measures of engagement that largely go unrewarded and unrecognized. Ideally, your engagement center should allow you to recognize these as well as online activities. To do so, however, you need an AMS that will measure and record traditional engagement using some sort of points system.

Lifetime Value 1.0 Versus 2.0 (Engagement, Engagement, Engagement)

As important as it is to measure, recognize, and reward all types of engagement, both online and offline, the next logical step is to consider how this strategy fits into the bigger picture of the Lifetime Value (LTV) of a member and the overall average LTV of your membership.

When most people think about the average LTV of their membership, they quickly try to calculate the average length of membership and multiply it by the average dollars spent by members in a year. This is a narrow way of viewing value. A member may have never attended a conference or event and simply paid annual dues, but does this mean they do not provide any other value to the community? LTV needs to be more holistic and embrace not just dollars spent but value provided.

LTV 2.0 is an emerging area that provides a more inclusive way of measuring who your most valuable members are. For example, I may have renewed my dues every year for the past 10 years with an average renewal price of $200 per year. LTV 1.0 would give me a value of $2,000. However, this doesn't take into account the five years I have served as a chapter officer, three years on a committee, or the articles I have contributed to the association's magazines and newsletters.

Now take this a step further and consider the emerging social tools available, such as blogs, wikis, eGroups, or file sharing. Engagement is not just about writing a blog; it is about all the associated activities, such as rating, commenting, reading, sharing, and other related actions. Creating is just one attribute surrounding a blog, but there are many more that can be measured and ultimately rewarded.

By collecting all the points from both your social platform and the more traditional engagement activities, such as chapter officer or committee volunteer, the society will be able to run reports to recognize their most valuable members for all their contributions, in both time and money. This more holistic view is LTV 2.0.

CHAPTER 12

Engagement 3—Demographics, Profiles, Blogs, and eGroups

Intuitively, we all know the truth of "birds of a feather flock together." When you are looking out over a mass of numbers and letters that represent your customer base, it is not always easy to see who is connected to whom, and seeing a clear pathway for influencing customers is not always readily apparent. One of the most critical pieces of social networking is the ability for users with common interests to connect. Grouping and the collecting and using of demographics are extremely important to your social network. If you are familiar with marketing basics, you might think this is just basic segmentation. It is. The only twist is that instead of trying to slice one large body of data into manageable slices, you start with discrete data and try to see connections.

Demographics

Demographics should be a primary consideration in your social strategy. Before diving in, it is important to understand how demographics are typically used. If you ask your marketing department, you are likely to hear a response along the lines of, "We use the various demographics to segment the membership and target-market them." In the majority of cases when I have met with associations and have delved into this question in more detail, it turns out that the demographics that are currently captured are not used at all. Targeted marketing is a nice idea in principle, but the reality is that most targeted emails are focused on location instead of other types of demographics, such as interest groups, Standard Industrial Classification (SIC) codes, and size of company. For example, many associations will send a blast email to only the tri-state area around New York City if a professional development workshop is being run in New York City. The assumption, in this case, is that the course is much less likely to attract members outside the local area.

Changing Value Proposition

The new era of the social web allows us to change the traditional value proposition of asking members for demographics. No longer do they have to think the only reason is so the association can spam them. Indeed, the new message to be delivered to the member is that updating individual and corporate demographics will increase their networking opportunities. Of course, it will still provide target marketing opportunities, but this becomes a secondary consideration, especially if this strategy was rarely used anyway.

If I am a member who works for a Fortune 100 company and I have updated my individual and corporate demographics, I might enter 30 fields of information, but every field can turn into a networking opportunity. For example, if I entered "Colombia," "South Africa," and "India" for the corporate demographic field of "countries with sales operations," the moment I click on SAVE, the system would dynamically look for other like members. If it finds at least one other member with either of those entries, it will build a network of like people. A network is simply a prefiltered search of the member directory (social network), and associations can have an unlimited number of networks based on any type of demographics they use.

Example of Demographic Networks

The following are examples of networks that are dynamically created when users update their demographics. Using the example below, you can see that none of my contacts (friends) have operations in Africa, but there are 648 others who do, bringing the total (including myself) to 649 members who have indicated they have regional operations in Africa. When clicking on any of the numbers, you are typically taken to the member directory (social network) search results.

Network	Type	Your Contacts	Potential Contacts	All Members
ADA Compliance	Interest	3	14	18
Africa	Operational Region	0	648	649
Alabama	Operation State	1	321	323
Alberta	Operation State	0	224	225
Alt. Risk Transfer	Interest	6	60	67
Asia	Operational Region	4	1586	1591
Australia and Oceania	Operational Region	3	1102	1106
Captives	Interest	4	42	47

Identifying Demographics

Before you can really figure out which demographics to capture, you need to understand which demographics are currently being captured, by whom, and for what purpose. This is often a time-consuming process and is not as simple as sending out a blast email asking the question. For a start, users need coaching about what demographics are and how they might be used. For example, if you asked your publishing department which demographics they capture, they might reply "none," but later you may find out that the auditors need to know specific information about the members and subscribers who receive the magazine so the magazine can pass its fulfillment audit. It is critical that these areas are identified, documented, and discussed. While investigating this information, use the opportunity to explain how demographics might be collected going forward. Ideally, at the end of this exercise, you'll have a centralized location for all demographics and a clear understanding of how and why they are used.

Examples of How Different Departments Might Use Demographics

Department	Use demographics to:
Meetings & Events	Demonstrate the buying power as well as the level of attendees. Used to track if the average seniority of an attendee is trending up/down.
Government Affairs	Help with lobbying by showing the types of companies which are represented such as "60 percent of the Fortune 500" or "100 companies with operations in South Africa with a collective annual revenue of $x bn."
Membership	Certain information required for the Membership Application approval process. Understand who the members are. What is the average age, gender, seniority, industries, interests, etc.? Used to identify trends to look for threats (e.g., aging membership) and opportunities (e.g., to engage students, provide mentoring)
Publishing/ Magazine	To sell print space in the monthly magazine. Advertisers need to know who is reading the magazine, and the demographics are usually taken into account as part of the annual fulfillment audit.

Unfortunately, with the above approach, the members' interests traditionally have been under-represented mainly because use of the demographics has not revolved around members before. The membership department is probably the right area to investigate what would be useful for members (taking into account the networking opportunities it provides).

Once all departments have been consulted and a final list of demographics has been created for both the company and the individual, you should end up with a list of all current demographics and an indicator of whether they are used, useful, or wanted. Combine this with the new list of demographics that the stakeholders want and then split them into two categories—corporate and individual—to end up with a final list of demographics to be integrated.

Corporate Versus Individual

Now that you have a list of all the demographics, it is time to decide how to manage both individual and corporate demographics. There is no right or wrong way to do this. Fortunately, the social web provides a new approach that traditionally has not been used, capturing both individual and corporate demographics at the individual level as part of their social profiles. When saved, the individual demographics would update the record within the association management system (AMS) if required (often not necessary, but it depends on how the demographics are to be used). When updating a corporate record, you need to decide if you will allow changes to update just the corporate demographic information tied to the individual or whether you want it to write back to the AMS and update the actual corporate record.

There are often sensitivities around this area. Some organizations allow any individual attached to a company to update the company record, while others allow only the priority contact. The primary contact is often one of the most senior people—often the one with the least time to do this relatively simple task. Depending on the structure of your membership and whether you have corporate entities as part of the membership, you might want to open up the demographic updates for the corporate record to anyone associated with the company. If necessary, you could set an automated alert to notify the primary person when there is a change and who made it.

There are many approaches to capturing demographics, including not using your social platform at all and just writing directly to your AMS. This is not supposed to demonstrate the "correct" way of doing it for all; it is merely to help explain how demographics can be part of your social initiatives.

Profile Completeness

The next step in your social strategy is to come up with a plan that will encourage your membership to fully update their profiles. A significant amount of the profile should be dynamically created from traditional engagement activity that is recorded in the AMS. For example: Events that a user attends, continuing education credits earned, location, job title, and so on. There are still many areas that are typically not stored in the AMS, such as the user's photo, bio, job history, education history, and certain types of demographics.

Completeness Indicators

If you are familiar with LinkedIn, you will be familiar with its "completeness" bar. To the end user, it might be just a helpful indicator of whether you have completed your profile. To LinkedIn, however, it is a tool used to encourage users to update their profiles. Here is an example of how this looks on LinkedIn:

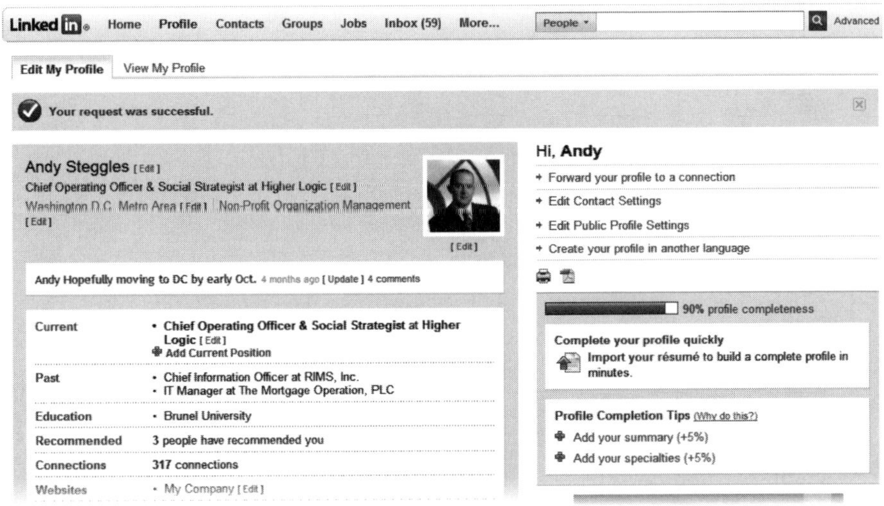

Notice the "90 percent profile completeness" indicator on the right side with profile completion tips below it. This is a very subtle way of getting people engaged by prompting them to update their own profiles. This will not work with everyone, of course. Many simply will not care. Conversely, there are a large number whose personality types make them care. Accountants, for example, are typically detail-oriented and tend to strive for perfection. If accountants see profiles that are only 90 percent complete, the odds are they will want to get to 100 percent and will take the extra effort to achieve this.

The Society for Corporate Compliance and Ethics (SCCE) decided to show a user's completeness in the main masthead of the website. This is significant because it means it is visible from every page. Since the notice is so prominent, they also include other key items that they want to draw attention to, such as the number of unread messages and a link to the communities section. The New York Society of Association Executives took a similar approach:

Components of Completeness

Gauging profile completeness may sound simple enough, but there is more in it than first meets the eye. For a start, what weighting do you assign each of the various elements that comprise the 100 percent completeness target? Do you assign 20 percent for the person's name, 40 percent for the photo, 30 percent for the address, and 10 percent for the phone number? There is no right or wrong answer, but here are a few things to think about while deciding about weighting:

Guaranteed Completed Elements

Which elements of the person's profile are already guaranteed to be in place? For example, when a user initially creates a profile, which fields are "required"? Let's say it is just the first name, last name, and email address. But if you have decided your platform is going to be exclusively for members, you know there will be no nonmembers logging in (because your system does not allow it). Then the question becomes what fields must be supplied for a person to become a member? For now, let's assume those fields are:

- First name
- Last name
- Email address
- Company name
- Work address (city, state, country, zip or postal code)
- Work telephone

In this example, we know with 100 percent certainty that every member will have these elements completed because they are required and membership will not be approved without them. The next step is to group all the "required" fields into something generic and assign a relatively low percentage (e.g., contact information: 10 percent), so you know every member will have at least this percentage complete when they start.

Assign Percentages

Decide how much of the percentage weighting are you going to allocate to the demographic fields because you want to separate each demographic or group of demographics to ensure they are complete. For example, you may decide that you are going to assign 60 percent of the completeness percentage to demographics alone. If you go with this approach and you have 20 demographic fields that you split evenly, each will receive 3 percent of the total completeness target.

Identify all the remaining elements that should make up the remaining completeness target and assign a percentage to each. So the total completeness distribution might look like this:

- Contact information = 10 percent
- Photo = 15 percent
- Bio = 5 percent
- Job history = 5 percent
- Education = 5 percent
- Demographics = 60 percent

Completeness Reporting and Component Buy-in

When you first implement a completeness tool or something like it, be sure to identify what the members' average completeness is. If this is a brand new platform, then everyone will likely start with just 10 percent completeness. If you were able to import some of the previous demographic answers, then you may have a higher number as the average completeness of members' profiles. Having these figures to start will help you demonstrate progress (or lack thereof) by benchmarking against yourself and will be useful for the marketing department, which should be helping you encourage members to update their profiles.

While the completeness average is a good barometer to measure progress, it would be wise to put together a more comprehensive report if you have the resources available. Such a report would show the number of completed profiles by percentage.

One association started to capture demographics in August 2009, when the average completeness of members was approximately 30 percent. Just over a month later, the report indicated the average completeness had risen by approximately 2.5 percent. This is significant because no real marketing effort had been implemented during that time. The progress was attributable mostly to the profile page completeness indicator.

Component Champions

In addition to working with your marketing department to put together a campaign to entice members to update their profiles and ideally reach the elusive 100 percent completion status, you might effectively push this initiative by requesting the help of your components. You can create a report ranking every chapter by an overall average for profile completeness. The association then can reach out to officers of each chapter with a link to the report and ask them to see how they ranked against other chapters.

This strategy usually helps improve overall completeness because chapters can be fiercely competitive. By showing chapter leaders the report and hinting that the average completeness "winner" would be recognized at the annual conference, the association encourages chapters to reach out to their members, asking them to update their profiles to help the chapter. This example uses chapters, but consider any other types of communities you might have, such as special interest groups or committees. Make completing profiles a mission of all the stakeholders.

Blogging Strategy

Blogs are a way for people to voice their views about anything. Many associations are now using blogs, and most are recognizing measurable success. Rob Price, director of web experiences for Meeting Professionals International (MPI) explains that MPI initially set an aggressive goal of reaching 500 blog additions or comments in the first six months after launch. They were pleasantly surprised when they reached 900 in the first three months from 150 different contributors. MPI has community and personal blogs, with an impressive mix of member/nonmember contributions that are attractive to members and open enough to attract nonmembers.

MPI's experience is contrary to that of Educause, which also launched member blogs. As Matt Pasiewicz, content program manager from Educause, says, "We know many of our members already have blogs, and this is one of our biggest challenges. Why should they stop blogging in their existing environment and move to our platform when they have already established a loyal following?" There is little incentive for them to do so. When considering offering your members a blogging platform, some thought should be given to how tech-savvy your membership is and what percentage of the potential bloggers have already started blogging elsewhere. Matt's comments highlight the risk of waiting to offer your members the ability to blog on your association website.

Many associations have dipped their feet into the water by allowing members to contribute (guest blog) to their association's blog. The problem with such a system is that it is association centric, not member-centric. A more forward-thinking approach would be to use a platform that allows any member to blog at will. The biggest fears about such an approach are related to negative or inappropriate postings. There are definitely ways to mitigate these risks, however. The legal obligations of the association have been more clearly defined in Chapter 7 of this book.

Member Blogs Versus Association Blogs

Rather than simply having a blog for your nonprofit, in addition (or instead) consider allowing members or donors to create their own blogs tied directly to their professional profiles. If you do not provide the platform, they will likely establish a blog on another platform where you have zero control. As Educause found, once members set up a blog on other websites, it is often too late to get them to create them on your website because every blog has an address. It is difficult to move a blog. Consider asking bloggers who have sites elsewhere to syndicate their blogs into their profiles on your website. If your blogging platform supports it, the member would simply log in and then add their RSS feed to their blogging profile. This means that when the member posts a new blog on their website, it automatically sends a copy of it to the association website. Not all member bloggers will be willing to do this because it diminishes the value of their own websites; on the other hand, the blog is getting much more exposure to a targeted audience than it may have otherwise.

Most associations are now using a more inclusive approach to blogging and allowing their members to blog in the association network. Associations should strategically leverage this user-generated content. For example, when creating a blog, the user should be able to associate the blog with a community and/or a tag. This is extremely useful when aggregating the blogs to display on different areas of the website in blogrolls. A blogroll is simply a list of the latest blogs which have been handpicked or dynamically created based on tags or communities. For example, if the Los Angeles chapter wanted to show "Latest Blogs" on its home page, it would use a widget to display a blogroll that is set to display any blogs associated with the community "Los Angeles Chapter." Similarly, the conference department might want to have its own blogroll that is set to include only blogs with specific tags such as "Conference" or "MWA 2010." Finally, the association might want a broader blogroll displayed on the home page of the website showing all the "Latest Blogs" without any filter.

Permissions

Just when you think you have a full grasp of all the issues surrounding blogs, you must think about permission issues. Some associations still have all blogs restricted to members only, and they consider them a member benefit. Generally speaking, this is a mistake for a number of reasons; here are the top two:

1. Members will be reluctant to blog if the blog is not going to get the exposure it deserves. Why would they blog on your platform where only the membership can see it, when they could blog on a public platform and the world can see it? It does not make sense.
2. The association should not dictate who can see the blog, the member should decide. (Think member-centric, not association-centric.)

The only person who should set the permissions for a blog entry is the creator. A member creating a new blog should be asked two questions:

1. Who should be able to view this blog?
2. Who should be able to comment on this blog?

If the member has posted a blog that is particularly sensitive, then he or she may decide to restrict that one entry to members. Generally speaking though, most bloggers select the public option, which means anyone, including the search engines, can view the blog. Commenting is a different ballgame, since you want accountability. Two options that are normally selected for who can make comments are "anyone logged in" and "members only." Some also just switch off commenting.

Members only blogs also present another potential problem. What happens if you have a blogroll for latest blogs, and someone posts a blog flagged "visible only to members"? Ensure your blogrolls take this into account and honor member-specific permission settings.

How to Deal with Negative Blog Postings

Traditionally there have been three ways of mitigating the risk of negative blog postings on private platforms:

1. Press Delete (traditional approach)
2. Ignore and hope there are no negative repercussions (usual approach)
3. Embrace (emerging and recommended approach)

Unfortunately, not everyone is comfortable with the embrace option, which is where you deal with something head-on by responding to the blog posting for all to see. Using blogrolls provides another option.

Instead of pressing the delete key, it is possible to simply suppress any specific blog from any and all blogrolls. This is very different from deleting a blog, as the blog will still exist, and you can still embrace it head-on. You have the right, however, to choose which blogs you want to appear in your blogrolls. If you choose not to include a particular blog, that is acceptable.

Anyone knowledgeable in the world of social media will always advise embracing controversy, with no hiding whatsoever. If someone posts something negative about the association, this is the time to get your side of the story across. Do not bury your head in the sand and think nobody will see it. Search engine bots are crawling your site every few minutes of the day, looking for fresh, new content.

The embrace option is the perfect solution because if one person has written it, another is thinking it, and this is your opportunity to spin the issue and address it. If the organization made a mistake, acknowledge it, say what you are going to do to ensure it does not happen again, and move on. Social media is all about transparency, and hiding someone else's content is something that really goes against the principles of the social web.

Nurturing Bloggers

If your members take the time to blog, ensure you thank them and recognize them not just on the web but also in printed media. (Profile a new blogger, for example.)

Moderator Options

Since moderating considerations apply to anywhere there is user-generated content, the principles in this section apply to blogs or eGroups. Regardless of the platform, where there is user-generated content (UGC), there are normally three options. If you're using a private platform, you get to choose the options; if you're using a public platform, they are usually chosen for you.

- No Moderation. Everything goes through without any staff review and no obvious option for recourse.
- Self-Moderation. Nothing is reviewed before being made public, but every posting has a link next to it that says, "Mark as Inappropriate"

or something to that effect. When someone clicks on this link, a pre-designated action occurs, such as removal from public view pending staff review.

- Full Moderation. Every posting is approved before being made visible to the public.

The legal implications of inappropriate material created by third parties appearing on your website are discussed in detail in Chapter 7 of this book. It is important to remember, however, that associations do have an obligation to deal with material that has been reported as inappropriate. Usually blogs, eGroups, and other areas with UGC are self-moderated and have some kind of button next to them to indicate it is inappropriate. Keep in mind that there is a difference between inappropriate (antitrust, slander) and negative (someone saying that the association is not serving member needs). Negative postings should be addressed, while inappropriate postings should be removed.

Discussion Groups (eGroups/Listservers/Forums)

There are not many strategic decisions with respect to setting up eGroups/listservers, or forums. The direction you take completely depends on your environment. The most important decision is to determine how many discussion groups to create and for which segments of the membership.

The number of groups to create may not sound like a difficult question, but it is a critical one that will have serious implications to the success of your social strategy. This is a balancing act between too many (not enough activity in the groups) and too few (broad conversation not targeted enough). Here are two scenarios to help give you ideas to think about when making these decisions:

Scenario 1

The association has 10,000 widget-maker members, and each member has one core area of expertise within the industry. The total number of expertise options is five. You have 50 state chapters that meet mostly to discuss nonlocalized widget-related issues.

This is a relatively straightforward scenario. You would create five discussion groups with approximately 2,000 people in each. You would not create discussion groups for the chapters because doing so would potentially dilute the conversation from the main five discussion groups.

Scenario 2

An association has 10,000 widget-maker members, and each member has multiple areas of expertise, indentified from a maximum of 30 areas. The average member has 10 areas of expertise. You have 50 state chapters that meet mostly to discuss localized legislation issues.

This is a more challenging scenario because you do not want to subscribe members to too many discussion groups, since the more groups there are, the less likely it will be for them to participate fully. In this example, I would recommend a single discussion group to encompass all areas of expertise and subscribe all 10,000 members. I would also create a discussion group for each chapter and subscribe the members to their respective chapter groups because the chapters have issues that relate only to their state and do not affect the rest of the society.

These two scenarios demonstrate the complexity of the decisions about how many discussion groups you create and who should be subscribed to them. Here are the most important considerations/recommendations:

1. Do not subscribe any single member to too many discussion groups. Too many usually is more than two.

2. Do not create a miscellaneous discussion group (such as "Widget Makers Discussions") as well as interest/industry specific ones. If you do, 90 percent of postings will be submitted to the generic group rather than the more targeted one. Select a single miscellaneous group or multiple targeted groups but not both.

3. Always auto-subscribe. If you create the discussion group and expect your members to subscribe, very few will do so. Subscribe them but ensure you incorporate a daily digest option and have a one-click unsubscribe feature.

4. Do not subscribe large numbers of people to receive real-time email. If you do this, many of your members will be displeased, and you run the risk of having your email server/IP address blacklisted. Unless it is for a small group such as a committee or task force, always use

the daily digest option that sends one email per day, collating all the messages posted into a single email.

There are always exceptions to these guidelines. I recently worked with an association that had approximately 10,000 members and four special interest groups (SIGs) that all had their own websites. In this example, they subscribed approximately 1,000 members to each of the groups and then subscribed the remaining 6,000 members to a single more generic miscellaneous group. The generic group was hidden from the SIG website, and the SIG discussion group was hidden from the main website where the generic group was located. This clearly goes against rule number 2 above, but the issues were clearly thought out and the justification was solid.

CHAPTER 13

Component and International Strategy

Everywhere we look, new niche social networks are emerging. Some are from start-up companies; others are from more established companies that are trying to diversify their offerings, gain customer loyalty, or simply reinvent themselves. For example:

- For-profit event companies are providing membership in their respective industry social networks as an "attendee benefit."
- Printed media (magazine publications) are allowing their readers to network as a "subscriber benefit."

Sermo.com is a great example of a for-profit start-up that has successfully established itself as a threat to traditional nonprofit medical associations. In the fall of 2006, Sermo raised $3 million in funding, followed by a further $9 million in early 2007, and then an additional $26 million in the fall of 2007 (http://www.sermo.com/about/press-releases). Sermo claims to be the largest online physician community in the United States, spanning 68 specialties.

Sermo should be seen as a wake-up call not only to the American Medical Association and each of the 68 (and growing) specialty associations that it now competes with but also to every other association. Sermo does not offer everything an association does, but it does offer networking and education, two of the key reasons why people join associations. Unlike most associations, Sermo does not charge a fee to join.

Social Saturation

With so many social networks, the threat of social saturation is real. At what point will there be so many social networks that none are relevant? This is definitely a real possibility in the public spaces, such as Facebook, LinkedIn, and Plaxo (among others). However, social saturation will be more difficult to achieve in private, niche networks because of pre-existing loyalty. The loyalty will last only so long before members give up waiting for their associations to provide the tools that other sources are offering for free.

This book has already discussed how the risk of for-profit social networks can be mitigated if the association implements its own social strategy, but now it is time to understand how associations and their affiliated or nonaffiliated chapters can work together to avoid social saturation, enhance the member experience, and collaboratively form their own "social network of social networks."

Community Management Challenges

Chapters, especially those run by volunteers, have long suffered from similar sorts of problems, mostly related to technology challenges. For example, managing a website with a constant turnover of member volunteers can be challenging at best. Updating the member database and making changes is difficult if chapters do not have a web-based database that members can use to update information directly. Chapters struggle with accepting meeting registrations and usually have no e-commerce payment system to receive payments for events. The latest challenge chapters are facing is what to do with social media and whether to set up their own social networks, as Florida Society of Association Executives (FSAE) and New York Society of Association Executives (NYSAE) have done.

All these problems present opportunity for the mother association to provide chapters with an integrated social platform and to prevent fragmentation. As traditional chapter staff or volunteers start to use Web 2.0 tools, they are starting to evolve into the next generation of community managers.

Chapter managers of tomorrow are our next generation of community managers. A year or so ago, you would have been hard pressed to find any jobs for an online "community manager." A search on the popular job search engine Indeed.com recently revealed 72 exact matches for "community manager" and more than 7,000 hits for the broader "all words" search for community manager.

Components As a Threat

So what do these external threats have to do with components? Most associations are still trying to figure out the best way to mitigate the risks of start-ups like Sermo but are not realizing that their chapters and components are facing similar risks. Localized groups are constantly cropping up on the public social networks and/or meet-up sites and are becoming an increasing threat. What may not be recognized is that the chapters themselves can be a threat to the association.

There are many different types and sizes of components. Special interest groups (SIGs), chapters, regions, cities/townships, committees, and task forces are just a few. In this section, traditional chapters will serve as the example.

Most chapters are geographic, based on state, country, or region. Some chapters are incorporated under the mother association, while others are self-incorporated. Many are governed under the mother association's bylaws, but some are not. From the perspective of the social web, none of this really matters. What matters is that chapters pose a threat to the "mother" association similar to self-formed LinkedIn groups, Facebook fan pages, or Ning.com based websites.

Chapters now have tools at their disposal to provide enhanced member benefits that extend beyond their traditional boundaries. With little effort, a chapter can form its own directory, discussion groups, and file-sharing system. Fortunately for the association, chapters who use public platforms to do this will share the same disadvantages as the public platforms they use (as discussed in Chapter 8: Public Versus Private Social Networks). Some more web-savvy chapters, however, are starting to recognize how easy it is to establish themselves using a private social network.

The NYSAE recently launched a new website with a fully integrated professional social network, eGroups, and resource libraries, together with videos and podcasts. NYSAE has special interest groups for technology, marketing, membership, and finance, each of which puts on regular educational offerings, the content of which is not usually location-specific but instead is industry-specific.

The FSAE has undertaken a similar overhaul and has recently launched a social network also. While neither NYSAE or FSAE are technically chapters because they are self-incorporated and are governed by their own bylaws, they do represent a localized version of the American Society of Association Executives (ASAE). It is irrelevant whether they are technically chapters. The point is the same. They are localized groups that have become exceedingly well equipped to grow outside their local area. NYSAE and FSAE now offer webinars, online networks, buyer's guides, podcasts, videos, and other online benefits that can be useful to association executives outside New York and Florida.

Of particular interest is the fact that the cost of offering such services is minimal. NYSAE covers the cost of its entire website and social network from a single sponsorship. FSAE is also taking advantage of sponsorships and advertisements. These associations have little overhead and yet are seemingly able to provide similar or better services than their national or international relatives. In this example, the real threat to ASAE is what happens if either NYSAE or FSAE reaches critical mass for little or no cost to the membership.

In these examples, the only thing that is really restricting the associations is their names (New York and Florida), and the words "Executive" and "Association." How long until one of them decides to rename itself to be more inclusive? In the association world, there has often been discussion about how ASAE's name is not inclusive enough because it focuses on America, associations, and executives, yet there are many members who are not executives, work for charitable nonprofits or societies, and are located outside of the USA. How long until a state association renames itself to be something much more inclusive without any geographic boundaries? What if one of these two entities renamed itself to something like the "International Society of Nonprofit Professionals"?

Even if you decide the risk to your association is not credible, at least practice the principles of enterprise risk management by identifying and monitoring this type of scenario for your industry or interest as a threat, albeit a low probability one.

Microsites and a Social Network of Social Networks

This is a good time to introduce the concept of microsites. Microsites are websites that are powered by the main association website. Many associations use this type of technology not just as an extended service to their chapters but also as a revenue generator, message delivery vehicle, and way to manage the brand. For example, the International Association of Administrative Professionals (IAAP) uses microsite technology to power 400-plus component websites. Volunteer webmasters manage the websites, but since they are all using a common, relatively simple platform, they can also learn from each other and, to a degree, answer each other's questions. Corenet Global, which represents the worldwide corporate real estate industry, is doing a similar thing for approximately 100 components. By offering the component webmasters a choice of carefully crafted designs, Corenet Global is using the microsites to control its brand. Each design is styled to complement the Corenet Global brand and also has the correct logo embedded within each design. RIMS is another good example; it provides five different designs with five themes for each design for its 80-plus components. The microsite technology has both a simple and advanced content management system to cater to all levels of volunteer or paid staff. Within two weeks of going live, 40 RIMS chapters had built themselves a fully functional, interactive website with the tools provided.

Microsites do not have just branding power, either; they are a great way to deliver structured content. Many associations that leverage microsite technology create designs that include certain links/buttons that cannot be removed by the chapter. For example, in the case of RIMS, since a person cannot be a member of the chapter without being a member of the association, they might want links on every website for "Join Today," "About RIMS," and perhaps "Member Benefits." By using something known as "syndicated content," the association can create pages on its main website that are used to populate every chapter website (so the content flows into the chapter website versus simply linking to it). By leveraging this type of technology, the moment there is a new member benefit for the organization, it is updated in one place that immediately displays on every component website.

Take syndicated content one step further with more dynamic content, such as a calendar of events, job bank, or latest blogs. All can be syndicated from the mother website. How you leverage this requires a strategic discussion at the main association level.

While branding and syndication are great reasons for using microsite technology, think about nondues revenue. Since you control the designs, you also control the banners and where they are placed. This is discussed in more detail in Chapter 15.

One final key component of this type of technology is the ability for the chapters to restrict any page to the various security groups such as chapter officers or members only.

When selecting a microsite technology, be sure to choose one that will fit the technology ability of your components. For example, SharePoint (MOSS 2007) has microsite technology, but in testing, RIMS found it was both too costly and too complex to be a viable option for its chapters.

Lead Generation through Contact Management

The mother association often knows nothing about prospects who attend chapter meetings. And local chapters may never learn anything about prospects who create accounts on the main association website to register for events or make purchases. This is really a lose/lose scenario.

After empowering your chapters to run their websites from your website (microsites), the next step is to consolidate many or all of the chapter membership databases into the main association database. Of course, it is unlikely chapters will do this unless you extend the value proposition. At a minimum, they will want assurance that at any time they can download the updated database of all their members and nonmembers. Since you are providing this functionality, you may also want to allow the designated chapter officers the ability to send a blast email to their membership using a template that they create as well as the ability for them to update records.

For example, when RIMS started to tackle microsites, the biggest challenge was getting the chapters to give up their Access database, their Excel spreadsheet, or, in some cases, their file cards. After showing them how they could retrieve their entire member database from their own microsite with a single mouse click, the chapters started to become more open to the idea. It took the better part of two years for the majority of them to adopt the centralized system, but the rewards were tremendous. If someone goes to the RIMS website, creates a profile, and purchases a book, that person immediately becomes a prospect of the local chapter. The chapter then sends a blast email using the built-in email management system, inviting new prospects to attend an upcoming meeting. Conversely, people who go to the chapter website and create a profile to search the member directory are immediately prospects for RIMS.

By leveraging next generation community manager tools, chapters and the mother association are able to operate from a single database. Doing so involves other business considerations. What happens when a chapter officer logs in and updates the address of a member? Do you allow it to be written back to the main association database, or do you just email the change to the records management department? How you deal with this really depends on your business rules. For example, in your association a change in city or state may require a change of chapter, which, in turn, may require a new invoice be generated by the association if it collects chapter dues.

Chapters can be a huge asset with member record updates. Since they are more likely than the mother association to actually know the individuals, they tend to get updates quicker than the main association does. Essentially, you can have every chapter helping update your records.

Community Event Management, Online Registration, and eCommerce System

Chapters want users to be able to register online for their monthly meetings, and they also want to be able to receive payments for these registrations in real time by credit card.

This is not as simple as it sounds, since there are many implications. For example, recently, Payment Card Industry (PCI) compliance has become a huge issue for anyone who processes credit cards. There is tremendous liability involved in the processing if it is not done according to PCI standards. This is not something you want to hand over to your components to worry about. However, the last thing the mother association wants to do is to start collecting event registration payments for chapter meetings. The accounting for multiple chapters would be challenging and time-consuming.

By using microsite technology, an association can embed an event management system (most microsite systems come with one) and use a third-party payment provider. With most modern community management systems, the chapter selects the payment provider of their choice (such as PayPal, Google Checkout, or Amazon's Storefront). When someone registers for an event, the payment is processed by the selected payment provider, avoiding all related liability of the chapter. Most payment providers are intelligent enough to notify the microsite registration system whether the payment was successful as well as return the user to the microsite on completion of checkout.

Think of the data that becomes available to the mother association by using a centralized event registration system. For the first time, the association has an accurate picture of how many meetings every chapter has as well as how many and how often members and nonmembers attend. A good event management system should allow the chapter officers to add people after the fact so the chapter officers can use the system as a permanent repository of their records.

Since all the events are in a single place, when staff views the calendars from chapters, they can with a single click change from viewing a single chapter's events to viewing all chapter and industry events globally.

Social Network of Social Networks

Microsites are an important consideration of your social networking strategy because you want to try to deter your components from creating their own, competing social networks. By leveraging microsite technology, you can extend your own social network into your microsites. Assuming all the chapters operate from the same database of the association, there might be 100 chapters, each with its own social network. You would decide if you want to filter each chapter to its own constituency or open it up to the entire database. If you did restrict it to the respective chapter members, then when you go to the mother association website social network, the entire network would be visible. The reality is that all of the profiles within the networks are populated from the same database, so if a profile is updated in one of the social networks, it is updated in all the rest. This concept is known as the "Social Network of Social Networks."

Keep in mind the features that social networks have, such as friending and blogs. Using blogs as an example, if a member of the New York chapter goes to that website and blogs about xyz, that is considered a community-based blog. When viewing the chapter website home page, it is best practice to show "latest blogs" which are blogs from that chapter, before showing blogs from the rest of the network (perhaps as fillers if there have not been any chapter blogs). This same concept is true with a calendar of events, discussion groups, and latest updates.

International Considerations

Associations and nonprofits that have components are usually, but not always, large; some are international. From the public network perspective, the important thing to note is that Facebook is not the dominant public social network around the world. The country you are trying to penetrate affects which social network you need to engage, so you will need to do your homework concerning the many options in use globally. Before examining your social strategy for components, it's important to take into account the various cultures of your members.

Organizations based in the United States should realize that the same rules do not necessarily hold true overseas. Culture affects the way we talk and communicate to our members as well as the tools and services we provide them. Ownership, volunteerism, and leadership are very different in other countries. Components often tend to be more independent and less willing to be governed by the mother association's bylaws (if applicable).

In Europe, strict data privacy laws prevent the exporting of data outside the European Union to a country that does not have as strict data privacy laws. Many Canadian associations are reluctant to use U.S.-based software companies because of data privacy concerns brought on by the U.S. Patriot Act, which allows the government to look at relatively secure/private data. Even subtle cultural differences can cause problems. For example, some Canadian members may take great offense if they are not invoiced in French and/or in Canadian dollars.

From a private social network perspective, there are many international considerations. Globalization, internationalization, and localization are not just about having a website in different languages; it is more about having a culturally sensitive website. Here are three of the most common internationalization considerations provided as examples of the types of things to be aware of when selecting your platform.

Date Formatting

This is something that people not based in the United States can be particularly sensitive about and is something even domestic organizations should consider. Even if your membership is U.S.-based, you may have someone outside the United States register for an event or purchase a product. Ensure your developers are building dates that are culturally sensitive. In other words, use an Australian date format for someone who is viewing using an Australian web-browser or a U.K. format for a U.K. web browser. Another, simpler way of dealing with it is based on the website. If you are looking at a U.K.-based site, then there is a reasonable expectation the site will have U.K. date formatting. This is acceptable as long as you display a sample date next to the text edit box, such as [__/__/____] 14 January, 2010. If you are not asking the user to input anything and are simply displaying a date, ensure it is spelled out. For example, "03 January 2009" or "January 03, 2009" is perfectly acceptable to anyone viewing a site, but "03-01-2009" or "01-03-2009" is not because of possible confusion.

Internationalization for Websites

Software internationalization is often referred to as I18N (the first letter I followed by 18 letters and ending with the letter N). In the computer world, before we look at what language is to be used, we look at the culture of that language, as in British English versus U.S. English. When we use a date culture setting for the same language it is called localization. For example:

en-US is "English – US"
en-GB is "English – UK (Great Britain)"
en-AU is "English – Australia"

An international website has both a site-based (SNAMA.org) and browser-based (Internet Explorer) language and culture setting.

Resource files are used by programmers who know what they are building may turn international and may need to be culturally sensitive. Envision a resource file as an Excel spreadsheet with a list of words under different columns that represent the different languages and their respective cultures.

This is used wherever you wish to display a phrase for which there might be differences between cultures. For example: If I view a site with the words "organization name," I would see exactly this on an en-US site. However, from an en-GB browser, I might see "organisation name." Note the culturally-sensitive spelling difference.

When programming the site, builders typically examine the software for culturally sensitive words, take them out of the code, and add them to a resource file. The resource file is simply a long list of words and phrases which are translated into different cultures and languages. When the interpretation takes place, the program typically checks to see if there is an en-GB resource file and, if not, it checks for an "en" file. If that does not exist, it will use the site default.

Keep in mind this gets even more complicated when you consider that for a single word, the order might be different in a given language. For example, a particular culture might say, "Registration for Andy Steggles," while another might say, "Andy Steggles Registration." This means the entire phrase needs to be an entry in your resource file, where the name is a dynamically translated variable.

Currency

Currency is less of an internationalization issue than a financial issue. If you take the traditional route and put the dollar sign in a resource file for en-US and put a pound sign for en-GB, this is fine except the US$50 will suddenly become £50. In other words, the sign has changed, but obviously the amount has not. You would typically get around this by not using a resource file for the sign and billing in only one language or by putting currency conversion amounts into a lookup table to be displayed with the appropriate culture sign. Dynamic conversion is an option, but keep in mind if the funds are received in a single currency, then the dynamic conversion might be different from your bank's conversion (best left to the bank to sort out).

CHAPTER 14

Mobile Membership

Over the last couple of years, significant changes in three key areas of technology have caused tremendous growth in the mobile marketplace. These changes produced the sudden increase to more than 58 million smartphones used in the United States today.

- High availability of faster wireless broadband
- Proliferation of mobile applications
- Significant improvement and availability of advanced-featured smartphones

It is not surprising that this perfect trifecta is trending to quadruple the size of the U.S. smartphone market to more than 160 million by 2013.

Mobile Membership

If 2009 was the year of social media, 2010 is most certainly the year of *mobile*. Already almost 50 percent of mobile users sleep with their phones nearby; 82 percent of Americans never leave home without their mobile phones; and 42 percent say they "cannot live without" their mobile phones![1]

As associations, we need to be where our members are, which is clearly on their mobile devices. But before we can begin to realize how to leverage this trend in the marketplace, it's important to understand the various flavors of mobile and how everything may not be how it first appears. Mobile integration is the very latest checkbox that many software providers are rushing to be able to check when responding to requests for proposals (RFPs), so understanding what "mobile compatible" means is key. There are two sides to this equation: mobile webpages and mobile applications.

Mobile Webpages

Almost any technology provider can tell you that their software is "mobile compatible" because almost any recently sold smartphone can view a webpage. However, it doesn't mean what is going to be displayed is going to be of any use because it may be difficult to read and may be terribly slow to download—too slow for most people to wait. Some companies do create a website designed to work with mobile devices, so the page is easily viewed (mobile-friendly). For example, if you view washingtonpost.com on a mobile device, the page is different than when viewed via a PC. In this instance, their site has been specifically configured and designed for mobile for quick, specific access. Mobile internet access can be extremely useful in certain circumstances, for things such as checking the status of your pending flight while on the way to the airport or checking on the latest headlines during the commute to work.

When looking at the vast array of information offered by an association website, it is impractical to try to create the same mobile version of the website for the entire portfolio of webpages. If an association goes the mobile webpage route, they really need to define which pages are a good fit for smartphones. For example, for an individual-based membership, the member application might be a good fit. Trade organizations, however, often have prohibitively long membership applications.

Mobile Applications

A mobile application is different from a mobile webpage because a mobile application has been created to run on a specific mobile device, such as an application built specifically for an iPhone, Blackberry, Android,

Symbian (Nokia), or Windows Mobile device. The benefits of running an application locally on the device primarily relate to usability and speed. For example, while the user experience may be more cumbersome when a user posts a message to peers via a mobile web page, a mobile application can relieve that burden by taking care of things such as spell checking locally and only communicating with the web server when necessary (thus reducing the bandwidth required, which has a direct impact on performance/speed).

Mobile applications are not just designed for a specific device. They are also designed for a specific purpose (member directory, newsfeed, events, for example). From a programming perspective, an application has much more flexibility than a webpage; therefore, the user experience is normally so much better than what the web has to offer. Due to security restrictions, webpages typically cannot interact with more advanced tools such as using a phone's GPS, camera, address book, or RFID. Mobile applications, however, have a different set of security protocols and most have full access to these tools. This makes the opportunities surrounding mobile applications much more interesting. Of course, not everything with a mobile application is more beneficial. For a start, you need a smartphone to use these purpose-built applications and when something is developed, it usually must be developed multiple times (one for each smartphone operating system and different versions thereof), a process that can increase costs significantly if you are building custom software.

When evaluating whether to create a mobile webpage and/or a mobile application, the two key differentiators to consider are your member's usability considerations and the speed of a mobile application. The speed of the mobile application is typically much faster than a mobile webpage. The ability for the device to leverage GPS, camera, and other capabilities is usually considered a secondary benefit rather than a primary consideration. Of course even with the fastest smartphone, the performance is ultimately dictated by the quality of the programming.

Mobile Application Development Considerations

Unlike mobile web programming, mobile applications have to be built with great care to maximize efficiency of bandwidth. Every bit and byte is critiqued by the developers for usefulness and checked for redundancy. As an example, when a regular webpage needs to display all of the messages posted by a specific member, the webpage may send something like the following to the server:

```
http://www.myassociationxyz.org/process.aspx?FindMember=12333
&GetMessages=True
```

Because bandwidth is at a premium with mobile devices, the same request for information from a smartphone might be reduced to something like the following, which reduces the number of bits (characters) that needs to be transmitted from 78 characters to 32 characters:

```
http://z5.us/p.aspx?f=12333&g=t
```

This intense scrutiny over bits and bytes means that programs are much more difficult to develop in the right way, which is why some applications can perform poorly compared to others with similar functions. When assessing partners to build mobile applications, go to a company with proven mobile expertise instead of your regular software developer that, although interested in dabbling in mobile technology is likely not familiar with all the intricacies that can make the difference between a widely used mobile application and one that is not.

Mobile Applications Versus Mobile Webpages

The consensus among industry colleagues favors mobile applications. Statistics recently released show that 3 billion apps have been downloaded from the iPhone App Store and the frequency in which they are being downloaded is increasing. It took approximately six months for the second billion apps to be downloaded and just a little more than three months for the third billion to be downloaded.[2] It's possible that in several years, mobile webpage technology may evolve and be able to compete better against mobile applications. A lot of technical challenges will have to be overcome before that happens.

Member Culture

Many organizations have struggled with how many resources to invest in the online presence because their members are often on the road and don't have constant internet access. While their members may not be able to jump on their computers to browse the association website, they may certainly be willing to view the latest industry news or perhaps register for the upcoming conference on a smartphone if given the option. This really comes down to the culture of the organization and getting to know your members. Often you'll hear concerns that an association's membership is "too old" to be concerned with smartphones, but consider that 36 percent of iPhone users are in the age range of 35 to 54 years old and 17 percent are 55 years old or more.[3]

After taking a closer look, many associations have found that their members are more likely to access the association from a mobile device than via a personal computer or laptop. The Mechanical Contractors Association of America knows contractors are not in front of laptops but they like smartphones and use them during the workday. The Medical Society of Virginia discovered medical students are typically tech savvy and often have smartphones and use them while studying as well as during work. In a trade association that does a lot of lobbying, members are executives who travel frequently on planes, have a lot of meetings, and could also be on the Hill for a fly in. Smartphones could be used for advocacy alerts and updates as well as to connect and find members who have limited time but are always available via their mobile devices. Members of the International Association of Administrative Professionals are typically in front of computers during the work day and don't travel as much but still want to use a mobile device to connect with others and conduct business.

Mobile Membership Mission

Any association adopting mobile technology should have a relevant mission statement. Mobile is essentially a tool to enable members to perform interactive functions. What functions do you want your members to be able to perform? Your tools should tie into the overall mission and vision statements of the organization. They should also tie into your social media strategy because social media is often tied to mobile applications and/or mobile webpages. The social media initiative is often a key component of whether your mobile mission is successful (depending on whether you have social integration and what functions you are offering to your membership).

Once you've identified the organization's mobile mission, it is often fairly easy to come up with a list of possible applications, but narrowing and prioritizing the list can be more difficult. When brainstorming with colleagues about which mobile applications you think would be most useful for your membership, consider the culture of your members and the overall mission of the organization. For example, if your organization's primary mission is to raise awareness of your industry and your members are of a younger generation, then you may want to consider an application that would allow your members to blog. The blogs themselves would support the mission by raising awareness and the membership adoption would likely be greater than that of an older demographic.

On the other hand, if the organization's primary focus is to provide continuing education and/or deliver continuous benchmarking data and your members are mostly accountants, then perhaps emphasis should be given to mobile education (videos, podcasts, quizzes) and a custom benchmarking application that depicts a real-time view of the state of the industry (combined with the ability for members to update their benchmarking information).

The challenge is to be innovative enough to come up with application ideas that will not just re-engage your membership but will also be compelling enough to make nonmembers want to join. When searching for ideas, the first place to look is your current website to see what you might want to reinvent in the form of an application. Remember, mobile applications can be much more functional than mobile webpages, so don't just think about reproducing the same functionality and features. Be creative and use this as an opportunity to re-engineer the respective processes. Examples of common areas that might be turned into applications are:

Traditional Process	Re-invented Application
Membership application	Change the membership application process and increase the number of completed member applications who would otherwise have given up when confronted with an overly complex application. Reduce from a five-page application to a half-page application. Get name, address, and basic demographic information (enough to decide their likely viability to be accepted as a member) and their payment information. Collect all the rest of the information after you've received the provisional application and their money. If it will help politically within your association protocols, call it a "provisional membership application" so it can be introduced as something new instead of a replacement for the more traditional online membership application.

Traditional Process	Re-invented Application
Industry news	Rather than update the latest industry news once per day or per week, do it continuously with a constant stream of news. For example, if you hire an external news clipping service to produce abstracts of the top 40 articles of the day that affect your industry, the news might typically be emailed to all the members after it is uploaded in the morning. With a mobile application, the 40 articles can be uploaded throughout the day and every time a member checks for "latest news" they will likely see more content. Of course, the email will still go out in the morning to those who want it, but for those who like to keep their finger on the pulse, the more real time nature could be an attractive proposition, since they associate receiving the latest information with the association.
Member directory	Forget the traditional way of finding members and their contact information. Consider upgrading the functionality so your member directory becomes a full-fledged professional social network. Use an application that allows members to find colleagues with similar interests, allow them to "friend" each other as well as view richer, more informative profiles.
Discussion eGroups	Usually one of the most popular member benefits are the organization's discussion groups. Perhaps create an application that will allow members to post questions or responses and at the same time, view other contributors' profiles.
Facebook or Twitter or LinkedIn integration	There are tremendous opportunities with all these outposts. For example, assuming your organization has a Facebook fan page, create a simple application that allows members to write on the wall or perhaps upload photos or videos (taken from their mobile cameras) to your Facebook page. This is a simple way of generating engagement from chapter meetings or industry events. Remember, every member can be a reporter if you make it simple enough.
Events	There are a ton of mobile applications that can be developed around events. Often the most highly prioritized would be those associated with revenue generation. Online registration is the most obvious but start thinking even more creatively. For example, specifically for its event, the American College of Cardiology recently released a mobile application that allows members to find exhibitors by keyword using the exhibitor directory application. When you view an exhibitor profile on the mobile device, you see not just company information but also product information, expo floor location, and links to the exhibitor's website. One area that didn't appear in the application is sponsorship opportunities. Why not include paid ads? There is more than enough room on many of the screens. The possibilities with events are endless. Using Twitter as the backchannel for sessions and the event as a whole is an easy win, but start thinking about other opportunities, such as an online session guide or the personalized event itinerary with selected sessions, scheduled exhibitor meetings, and so on. When considering events, think about nonattendees and nonexhibitors. Are there any win-win opportunities around this area? Perhaps the exhibitor directory could be made available to the nonattendees, with one or two live streams of sessions that are broadcast. Shy away from the concern that people won't attend the conference if they can get it all online. They don't need to have it all online—just offer enough to get them interested, maybe one or two sessions per day. Remember, the mobile application can't replace the face-to-face networking, which is usually the primary reason most people attend.
Career center	Often, the most frequently visited portion of an association website is the job bank. Why not have a career center application for mobile devices? It could be as simple as an RSS feed that sends all the latest job postings to members on their mobile devices.

Mobile Engagement

The next step is to encourage engagement. Remember, mobile is anytime, anywhere and members do not have to be chained to a desk or be in person at an event to be active. Did you know that people who use Facebook on their mobile are twice more active on Facebook than non-mobile users?[4]

A mobile application is perceived as a much more personal experience than a traditional webpage. Even though this is not necessarily true, the perception of a traditional webpage is that it is designed for a one-to-many experience. Conversely, the perception of a mobile application is that because it is on your own smartphone, it is designed just for you, since the device itself is considered a much more personal asset of the individual. With this in mind, ensure your application is personalized by using a "My" approach to your apps—My News, My Events/Sessions, My Contacts/Friends.

Provide some kind of daily hook to get users into the habit of checking your app: industry news, contact/friend status updates, member-to-member notifications (contact requests, community invitations, direct messages). Be sure they can see what their peers are doing.

Remember, your organization's mobile app will often be perceived as the gateway to a professional social network, so members must be able to easily network, connect, and communicate.

Measure Engagement

Once you've decided which applications to build, consider how to measure engagement. At some point, you'll need to quantify the application's return on investment, including continued maintenance fees and support costs. As a result, the application should record its own activity data and pass it to your webserver and/or association management system (AMS) periodically. These statistics will allow you to measure how much the application is being used and by whom. You should be able to tell who your most active mobile members are, which will allow you to recognize and reward them, promoting further engagement.

Think of creative ways to recognize your most engaged members. Consider highlighting "Mobile Member of the Month" or something like that as a key feature of your mobile membership directory. Also try to tie your engagement/recognition strategy into more traditional media such as your monthly magazine or newsletter.

By recognizing the individual with the most engagement, there are benefits for both the individual and the association:

- For the individual, being recognized publicly in the association's website, magazine, or mobile membership directory may give them more exposure and name recognition to other professionals in their respective industries. Most people like to be recognized for being a thought leader in their industry, so this recognition gives them even more affinity to the association. Raising their profile within their industry also raises their profile within their peer groups, resulting in further career development opportunities for the individual (being asked to participate on different industry task forces, article submissions, and book deals).
- For the association, highlighting awareness about individuals and their increasing engagement, gives more publicity to the association's mobile application. Increased awareness about members' usage will spark curiosity among others in the industry about your mobile application, increasing its usage and the overall engagement within your target population.

Measuring engagement is easier said than done. Many associations are struggling with this now. When asked how much activity their membership directory/social network has generated, one might immediately think of how many searches have been performed or blogs posted. As discussed in Chapter 11, there are so many more activities than this, though. For example: number of friend requests, profiles updated, and communities formed, etc.

Whichever mobile applications you decide to build, be sure they measure everything possible, not only to prove return on investment but also to benchmark against past performance, so you know if your engagement strategies are working.

Mobile Application Provider Considerations

When exploring mobile applications, start with baby steps and avoid custom software. Use an out-of-the-box product that will perform the most commonly requested functions. For example, most associations would want to provide a member directory, news feed, event calendar, and a messaging service to their members. An off-the-shelf mobile application should be able to plug directly into your association management system (using web services) and distinguish between members, nonmembers, committee members, chapter officers, event attendees, and so on as well as personalize content.

A fully integrated mobile application may cost as little as a couple of hundred dollars per month for a small organization. This relatively inexpensive solution will give you not just an iPhone application but also applications for the other popular smartphones like Android, Blackberry, Symbian (Nokia), and Windows Mobile. The price typically scales with the size of the organization or its membership, meaning a mobile initiative is affordable for all. Costs can often be recovered in new advertising opportunities. When you have your mobile application set up and have proved its effectiveness, then start thinking about custom applications, such as your membership application or benchmarking tool.

References

1. http://bit.ly/synovateonmobile.
2. http://tcrn.ch/appstorestats.
3. http://bit.ly/mobdemo.
4. http://bit.ly/fbkstats.

CHAPTER 15

Nondues Revenue from Social Initiatives

One of the most effective means of generating nondues revenue is from subtle embedded advertising within emails. Many associations, including ASAE, are doing this now with their e-newsletters. Newsletter banners are particularly attractive to advertisers when the newsletters themselves are targeted toward a subset of the membership. Each community could have a sponsored newsletter. This is a simple example, but there are more innovative ways to make new revenue from social initiatives.

eGroups (Discussion Groups/Listservers/Forums)

Many associations already provide some kind of listserver as a member benefit. Listservers tend to have a love/hate relationship with association members. Members get frustrated with the "digest within a digest" issues from people replying to a single email in a digest but forgetting to remove the rest of the digest. Poor subject-line descriptions from people replying to the digest without changing the subject line are also a nuisance. Embarrassing emails sent to the entire listserver instead of the individual person, spam, out-of-office messages, and so on also cause concern. Over the years, some associations tried to address these issues by moving to online forums. This was usually not successful because the forums were not as proactive as the listservers; they did not typically send email digests. Many associations that moved to forums, saw a sudden drop in traffic because the assumption that readers would visit the website every day to view the content was flawed.

Consequently, a compromise of the traditional, proactive listservers with the high functionality, web-based forums was created. eGroups operate like listservers except for some key features. One of them is the fact that the emails generated are HTML-based so they actually look like webpages that are delivered by email. Essentially you are delivering emails in the same format as the email newsletters that you may already be sending out.

If this is the case, why not embed advertising in these emails as well? That is what a number of associations are now doing. Every time a member posts a message, the emails that are sent out to the membership at large contain subtle, nonintrusive sponsorship or advertising. No longer do you need to wait another month or two before the next newsletter is ready; you can now generate new revenue every day.

When launching eGroups, a best practice is to avoid putting advertising or sponsorship in the email to start with, but instead to use the ad space to promote your own products and services. Once members are used to the new format and the embedded ads for your own products, then slowly start replacing them with ads. By the time you do this, vendors likely will have contacted you asking about this new opportunity.

So how much do you charge for this new ad medium? A simple answer is to look at how much you charge for advertising in your newsletters if they are targeted to the same group. Models for charging differ based on the frequency of postings and the size of the egroup.

For example, if you have a group of 2,000 people in a single community and the eGroup is fairly active, with messages posted an average of five days per week, then you might want to consider charging 10 cents per subscriber, per day. In this instance, one week's advertising would work out to be:

$0.10 (10 cents) × 2,000 (subscribers) = $200 per day

$200 × 5 (days) = $1,000 per week in new revenue

Calculated over an entire year, the potential nondues revenue is impressive.

If you had a community of 500 people that was not very active and had only one or two postings every other week, then you might want to take a different approach to selling advertising. It is difficult to charge per week or for any short time when the frequency of postings is so limited. For smaller or more targeted eGroups you could adopt a flat fee over a longer time, using historical data to "guess-timate" (with no guarantee) how many messages will be generated. In this example, you might work out something like the following:

Two messages every other week = approximately five messages per month, 30 messages per six months or 60 messages per year.

> $0.10 (10 cents) × 500 (subscribers) = $50 per day
>
> $50 × 30 (days where there is at least one message) = $1,500 for a six-month sponsorship

There are different pricing models, including pay-per-click or per opened email. Of course, not everyone charges 10 cents per subscriber either; some charge more or less, depending on the perceived value of the eGroup. Consider this: If you were a vendor trying to sell to one of ASAE's listservers, such as Technology, Marketing, Finance, or Executive, how much would you pay for access to these specific market segments?

If your association does not have the resources to sell this new type of offering, consider outsourcing the sales to a third party. Normally, there is a split, or at least a commission, of revenue on anything they sell, but it is still better than nothing. To see an example of eGroup message with embedded advertisement, go to http://bit.ly/egroupexample.

Community Revenue

The social web provides all kinds of evolving and interesting nondues revenue opportunities surrounding communities. Of course, much of it depends on how active the community is, how targeted it is, and the level and number of subscribers attached to the community. The following examples are special interest group (SIG) communities that are using eGroups and have their own microsites and associated resource libraries. Using these parameters, below are opportunities for new revenue.

Increased Search Engine Exposure

If a community decides to have its own website, search engines will find and index it, members of the SIG will visit it, and over time it will gradually build up a history of content that will increase search engine exposure all around (for the areas that are not restricted to community subscribers only). The increase in search engine-generated traffic provides a good opportunity to increase the attendance at meetings, recruit members, and better overall retention through an increased overall level of community engagement (assuming the community is active).

Community Banners

When sponsors ask associations for advertising at the grass roots level, associations can finally say yes. As a reminder, a community can be a chapter, SIG, committee, or any other type of group. In this instance, we are looking at a SIG that has its own microsite, eGroup, and resource library. By using microsite technology, the association can place banners strategically on all chapter websites. When RIMS created its microsite designs, it reserved specific areas of the designs for banners. The RIMS strategy was to allow banners in the right hand column. The association could allow the chapters to upload their own banners and have nothing to do with the banners or the associated revenue. Another option would allow the association to place all the banners and either split the revenue with the chapters or keep it. RIMS came up with a compromise. RIMS does not charge its chapters to use the Microsite technology, and splitting or prorating revenue with the chapters would be overly complex and have little benefit. As a result, RIMS decided that the top two banners in the right-hand column would be owned by RIMS, and the chapter could have as many banners as it wished below them. If the chapter did not upload any banners, then more of the RIMS banners would show. In addition to this, RIMS reserved a banner advertising area in the left-hand column, under the left navigation for interior pages, which it used mostly for internal promotions, such as annual conference registration and a member-get-a-member campaign.

The way the system was set up, RIMS had to change the banners in only one place and the changes would immediately be reflected on all chapter websites.

Partnership Opportunities

Custom News Service

Have you ever considered subscribing to a custom news service for all or part of your membership? Many associations do this and achieve great results. Instead of paying people to write industry news, consider paying people to create executive summaries of the top articles and collate them into a weekly or daily executive briefing service. Busy executives often do not have time to read all the relevant industry publications but still want to be apprised of what is going on within the industry. Associations can fulfill this need by contracting with a company that specializes in this service, such as Information, Inc. or MultiView Inc. An association that pays approximately $100,000 per year for a daily news brief service might manage to raise $200,000 per year in annual sponsorships.

Open Archives

When selecting your vendor, pay attention to who will own the data and to the flexibility you have with opening the news to the public. For example, if you allow the search engines to crawl news archives that are more than six months old, there is still tremendous value with the search engines. All the less frequent key words that sites are not typically optimized for, do attract a significant amount of traffic (known as the "long end of the tail"). Opening archives is almost guaranteed to generate a lot of new search-related traffic that will increase banner advertising revenue and perhaps generate new members.

Job Bank/Career Center

If you currently have chapter websites, take a look at how many advertise local jobs. Then look at how many of these jobs are only in the chapter website and not in your job bank, assuming you have one. Job banks are a tremendous revenue stream, but the potential value can be diluted by the actions of the chapters. For example, say that an association averages 30 jobs per month at $200 per listing, netting an average annual revenue of approximately $72,000 per year. If that same association has 100 chapters that average one job per month on each of their websites but which are not also listed in the main association job bank, then there are another 100 jobs per month which could be in the job bank, adding to the member benefits that are already provided. Instead of generating $72,000 per year for 30 jobs per month, the association could potentially generate $312,000 per year for 130 jobs per month.

The for-profit job banks recognize the value of this model and have many similar networks. Until recently, however, mother associations have typically had little, if any, control over chapter websites and so have had little leverage. Talk to your job bank vendor about integrating your job bank into the chapter microsite technology. When chapter websites are designed, consider doing a revenue share on any jobs posted on chapter websites. This can be enforced since the "Career Center" or "Job Bank" button on all 100 of the chapter websites can be set so the chapter cannot move or hide this prominent link.

Other opportunities in this area include charging recruiters to access the professional social network directory to search for potential talent. Rather than making the job bank for members only or open to the public, try a hybrid approach, with jobs available to the public (nonmembers) 30 days after being posted and being open to members immediately. If a nonmember wishes to view the jobs, charge them perhaps $40 per month to do so.

Buyer's Guide

Any third-party platform, whether it is a buyer's guide, job bank, legislation system, or any other, can generate revenue. In this example, the buyer's guide demonstrates the point. A traditional vendor directory or buyer's guide is a list of companies and, optionally, their products or services, which are categorized. Companies pay to be in this online directory and usually have opportunities to purchase additional categories that they may wish to be found under. The price for a buyer's guide listing typically may be $400 per year for the listing and an additional $200 per extra category. On top of this, the company may pay to appear in a premium position in the search results.

An association that had been generating $15,000 in revenue from its in-house buyer's guide saw the revenue go up to $280,000 within three months of outsourcing it to MultiView, Inc. (a for-profit buyer's guide company). Even though the vendor typically keeps a significant portion of this new revenue, the association would still net a lot more revenue than they did previously.

Regardless of whether you outsource, the opportunity lies in the microsite technology. If your association powers 100 websites, and you have configured them all to display a prominent button for "Buyer's Guide" (or "Job Bank," etc.) that points to the same list of vendors, then any advertiser who pays to be in the guide will be listed in 100 websites. This additional exposure will be tracked by your vendor, who should be able to tell you how many hits were generated from which chapters. As always, the association decides whether to share any of the new revenue.

Community Webinars

Consider partnering with your advertisers to provide a series of webinars for your members. Community-specific webinars are often less expensive to run and are a great way of fostering the value of the community and ultimately generating engagement. For example, if a community of aircraft-specific widget builders is presented with a webinar, the webinar can be archived in the community resource library. A recording of the audio can be provided as a podcast, and the presenters can be asked to write blogs or articles about the topics they covered. The Health Care Compliance Association (HCCA) used this approach and arranged for speakers to answer a community Q&A session via their eGroups over a specific time. It is not uncommon for a webinar that is presented to 100 people to be sponsored for $1,000. The cost for the webinar could be as little as $200, depending on which vendor you use and how it is presented.

Listening

For-profit communities, such as Sermo.com, use a business model that revolves around companies' paying for access to the data Sermo collects, essentially paying to listen to the conversation. The Forrester Research book *Groundswell* (Forrester Research, Inc., 2008) documented a great example of this. The marketing person in charge of the BMW Mini brand was looking for alternative marketing ideas. This person commissioned a community of enthusiasts to collaborate, talk, and discuss their experiences with their beloved Mini cars. As a result of monitoring the conversation, the marketing person decided not to pay to advertise to non-Mini owners (like any other car company would instinctively do) but instead to market to existing Mini owners. They realized by monitoring the conversation that the best sales leads they could generate were word-of-mouth referrals from existing owners.

When you look at your communities, consider whether there is any value in charging vendors to access and listen to the conversation (you can enable them to listen but not participate) or charging them to conduct a survey for their marketing research.

Other Opportunities

Video Advertising

Vendors often ask associations if they can sponsor educational sessions at a conference. For most, the answer is a resounding no. With a little creative thinking, however, there are opportunities. One association that had a strict policy came up with the idea of not allowing the session to be sponsored but allowing the video recording of the session to be sponsored. The exhibitor picked three sessions from the conference that perfectly matched their product suite and paid $15,000 to sponsor the recordings. In return, the sponsor received a 10-second video advertisement that was played before the online session playback for three months. The cost to the association to have the sessions recorded by their A/V vendor was approximately $6,000. The net revenue from this simple example was $9,000, with little effort required from the association.

Pay Per Subscription

If all your communities and their respective components are members only, consider allowing a temporary pay-per-access model. This does not necessarily dilute the value to the membership. On the contrary, this can help demonstrate the value by assigning an actual dollar figure. You can limit the length of the access for which a nonmember can pay. For example, nonmembers can pay for access for no longer than six months, after which they must become members. By this time, the community value will have proven itself, and they will have no problem becoming members, especially if you offer to credit their $200 six-month subscription payment toward their membership dues if they join before the fourth month has begun (or something similar to this). Other opportunities for paid access include the custom news service and webinars.

Conference Session Recordings

It is reasonably easy to have all of your sessions recorded these days and the cost is minimal. For example, it might cost $5,000 for 70 one-hour sessions over a three-day period. Usually, you have collected all the sessions' presentations and handouts in advance as well. If you have the two, then you might want to upload them into an event-specific community where all members can have full access as an attendee benefit, or you can charge nonattendees for access. In any event, having a library with this educational information is extremely valuable even if you don't charge for it.

Dues/Retention

Although this chapter is focused on nondues revenue opportunities, keep in mind that many of the opportunities rely on a community's having a reasonable level of engagement. This means that you need to ensure it is successful by assigning the right community manager to help nurture it. On the plus side, if you are successful, you will have an actively engaged community. Engaged members will mean improved retention and a greater number of new members from word-of-mouth as well as from increased search engine exposure and the other nondues revenue discussed above.

Sponsorship Versus Advertising

One important consideration is the difference between sponsorship and advertising. You should check with your accounting office or tax advisor about the rules because you may have to pay tax on advertising versus sponsorship. What is the difference between the two when talking about banners or text ads in emails? The difference used to be determined by whether the graphic was animated or not.

CHAPTER 16

Private Social Platform Selection

An onslaught of social networking platforms has showered the association and nonprofit market. As a result, the most common questions are, "Which platform is the best?" and "How do I select a platform?" Unfortunately, it is not a case of one solution fits all, as every association is different. You must take into account numerous considerations. The following is a guide to navigating through the social platform selection terrain.

Why Use a Social Platform?

Many associations want to use the social web to satisfy the desire to provide advanced networking tools for constituents and to be the first to establish a professional network for their industry. While these are the most common reasons for wanting a social platform, other avenues may lead to social initiatives. Nancy Ostin, director of membership & marketing, of the Society of Naval Architects & Marine Engineers (SNAME), had a different approach. She was definitely not looking for a private professional (social) network; instead, she was looking to fulfill a list of core requirements that had been assigned to her by the SNAME leadership. Some of the requirements included:

- Provide a pay-per-view search-enabled tool to provide access to an archive of more than 10,000 historical documents that have been scanned and converted into text-recognizable PDF documents.
- Enhance the networking capabilities of the association's website.
- Grow awareness of the profession and the society with the younger generation.
- Establish an "Expert Directory" of the association's more learned professionals.
- Provide microsites for the association's 180 worldwide sections.
- Support scholarly excellence and recognition.
- Generate nondues revenue by leveraging Web 2.0 technologies.
- Provide support for their mentoring (and reverse mentoring) program.

After doing extensive research, Ostin arrived at the conclusion: An enterprise professional (social) platform that plugs directly into the SNAME association management system (Avectra's NetForum) was a natural fit. The historical archive could be indexed by resource libraries that allow members to not just purchase but also provide feedback (rate, review, comment, blog, and link). The integration with netFORUM was also a key component, since the resource library needed to know whether the user had paid to view a document. If not, there needed to be ecommerce integration between the two to allow for the purchase of a particular manuscript.

The discussions, blogs, and profiles contain a careful mixture of public versus private content and were carefully orchestrated to take advantage of the search engines. This has resulted in a significant increase in the number of pages and better positioning within search engine indexes. The expert directory was simply the public side of the member directory, populated by only those members who paid the additional $25 per year to be in it.

Ostin aptly named the entire scope of the project "Project Voyager," and it was tasked to touch all aspects of the SNAME member experience. The platform officially went to "sea trials" in early 2009 and has been embraced by both the leadership and membership at large.

Many associations and nonprofits are finding social platforms along this same route: They are not looking for a social platform per se. They are looking to fulfill a need, and leveraging the power of the social web is often found to be the solution.

Selecting a Social Platform

When looking for a social platform, try not to focus on all the features the platform offers because you may not use many of them. Focus on what you are trying to achieve from both a business perspective and a member benefit perspective and ensure those objectives tie into your mission.

The following are key considerations for selecting a social platform. It is important to note that there are many more considerations than these, but the following are the most important:

10 Keys to Success in Selecting the Right Social Platform

1. Security

When evaluating the permission structure of your platform, the first thing you need to decide is how complicated you need it to be. As with all these things, you will find that 80 percent of what you want will fit into most platforms with relative ease. However, it is the 20 percent that can lead to major problems. How important are these exceptions to the rules? Here are some ideas about the various levels of permissions:

a) **Member Types:** Can the platform distinguish between all different member types that are pulled straight from your AMS?

b) **Member Type Groupings:** Does the platform recognize groupings of constituents such as "members," "nonmembers," "associates," and so on? You might have 30 different member types, but you do not want to check a box next to every one that is considered a member every time you perform a simple task. Grouping of member types makes much more sense.

c) **AMS-Based Communities:** Can your platform provide permissions around other pre-established groups, such as committees or chapter officers or chapter officers with specific roles, all of which are normally stored in your AMS? You do not want to duplicate the permissions; they need to be inherited from your AMS so you edit them in a single place.

d) **Permission Types:** For each type of security group, can you set different levels of permissions, such as no access, read only, edit, create/write?

e) **Permission Hierarchy:** Is there a hierarchical structure to the permissions? For example, if you set up a community with a discussion group and resource library, will the features of the community inherit the same permissions as the community itself (and preserve the integrity)? If so, can these permissions be overridden by staff? As an example, if I have a community for our Quebec chapter officers where the permissions are actually inherited from our AMS roles, suppose the Quebec chapter wants to add someone to their group who is not a member (such as a paid administrator). Does your platform have this flexibility? More to the point, do you want to have this flexibility (as this could compromise the integrity of the security)?

f) **Security Trimming:** One problem with SharePoint (MOSS) is the inability to switch off security trimming. Security trimming is supposed to be a nice feature but really does not work well with nonprofits. For example, if I have a job bank that is members only, I may well be a member but will not see the job bank at all (not even the navigation item pointing to the job bank) until I am logged in with permissions to view it. This does not sit well with nonprofits because we need to show our prospective members what is available if they join. We do not necessarily need them to see the content of the job bank, just that it exists. The same is true with the social platform. You want the world to see many areas that exist while not revealing the content. Do not take it for granted that your platform can do this. As I discovered with MOSS, the feature could not be turned off, so I had to work around it.

g) **Components:** Will the platform provide permission inheritance down to the component level? What if someone is a "friend" of the chapter but is just considered a nonmember by the association? A community-based security schema would provide the flexibility to work around this issue. Is this something you need to be concerned about?

h) **RSS:** Are the platform's RSS feeds individualized? This is important in light of all the above considerations. If I do not regularly visit the site but have subscribed to RSS feeds to send me updates to discussions, libraries, and similar features, how will the system know if I should still have access? The only way is to personalize the RSS feed. Bottom line: Ensure that after someone has failed to renew, they can no longer pull the feed that they subscribed to while a member.

2. Integration with Your AMS

For most associations, this is a simple decision—yes. There are so many advantages to having AMS integration that it almost always makes sense, unless, of course, you do not have an AMS. For example, a small association may use an Excel spreadsheet or Access database to manage its members. This being the case, integration is not really a viable option. However, you can still provide your members their own social platform that will allow them to update their profiles and supply you with dynamically updated data. The downside to this is the complexity of keeping the data in sync. You need to decide which will take priority—the social platform for individual member information or the spreadsheet for dues. So long as you can download all member information at any time, it should be possible to import and update your home-grown system.

It is almost always worth integrating with your AMS because this is where your number-one strategic advantage is over LinkedIn and Facebook. Think of the wealth of information you have in your database that can be used for networking and community building. For example, when you look at another member's profile and the system tells you, "You may remember Rob from the 2003 New York professional development course on claims management." Perhaps you do not know the person, and instead the system suggests things you have in common like corporate demographics. (You work for companies with similar SIC codes or both have operations in China.) These are simple ways in which existing data can complement a professional network. In many respects, it is easier to try to pick the member information that cannot be used for your network, since almost all of it can.

3. Levels of Integration for Leveraging

Be careful when you approach a vendor and ask if they integrate. I have yet to meet a vendor who would say no. The key is to identify the level of integration and then ask to see examples and speak to clients whose websites they are demonstrating. The simplest and easiest form of integration is called Single Sign On (SSO). With SSO, the user can log in on one site and be recognized as logged in on the other. With most platforms, you will have your regular website, such as www.RIMS.org, and a sub-site for the social network, such as community.RIMS.org. The ability to log in on one and be recognized on the other is paramount to meeting usability expectations from your members. Multiple logins are frustrating, especially if you have extended the platform to your components. SSO is the simplest of integrations because all it does is validate your credentials and remember you. There is so much more to integration, however.

The most common elements to look for revolve around demographics and events. Typically you would capture individual and corporate demographics when you ask industry- and interest-specific questions as well as questions that relate to the buying power of the individual or the organization (to help with sales). In the past, this has been a one-way request; we ask the user to give us a great deal of information and, in return, we are able to more accurately email—or spam—them. Not exactly a compelling argument to get your members to update their demographics, is it? With the social platform, the game has changed. Now we ask our members to improve their networking opportunities by fully updating their profiles, in which most of the demographics reside (except for more sensitive things like race, year of birth).

Now, when I view my professional profile and select social media as a core interest, the moment I hit save, the system looks for any other like-minded people (anyone else who has made the same selection) and builds a dynamic network among the people, providing a great networking opportunity for all with this common interest. The same principle applies when you select your designations (group all those with a CAE or CMP, for example).

These networking opportunities exist only if you have a deep level of integration. Similar examples exist around events and professional development as well as legislative and volunteer activities. The opportunities are endless once you start reflecting on your in-house data, most of which is rarely used.

4. Vendor Evaluation

As with any platform selection, the vendor should be carefully scrutinized. In the same way you would question an AMS vendor's experience in providing member management software services in the nonprofit space, you should most definitely question two key elements for the social platform:

a) What is their experience in the nonprofit space?

b) What percentage of their business deals with the social web?

You can ask the question however you wish as long as you end up with a high level of comfort with their understanding of the nonprofit sector and the social web. Examples of competency indicator questions include:

a) Do they know the difference between a 501c3 and a 501c6?

b) Do they understand the importance of the volunteer leadership structure and their respective roles (committee officers, chapter/section officers, board, executive committee)?

c) Do they fully grasp the compromise we are all trying to reach of retaining member benefits versus giving away enough value to entice new members to want to join to get more?

Many companies are trying to break into the nonprofit market. Often they end up abandoning the market because of long lead times and inability to push their clients forward in the decision-making process. Any company that is experienced in this area would be more understanding of the typical bureaucracies that nonprofits employ, such as volunteer structure (committees, boards, chapters, sections), high level of due diligence, and lack of overall urgency or concern about time to market, which for-profits typically experience.

Recently, I heard of one vendor asking a prospect to sign a letter of intent and another that offered a steep discount if the association signed by a certain date. These tactics typically do not work in the nonprofit market and only highlight the vendor's inexperience in this sector. (Usually senior staff or the board will not be pushed into making a decision.)

A vendor's experience in the social platform market should speak for itself. Assess what percentage of their business is focused on the social platform. For example, if they are an event management company or an

AMS provider that just happens to have a free social networking platform, it is likely that their solution is not a best-of-breed one and will have the bare minimum of features. On the other hand, a company that focuses on nothing but social platforms is more likely to be feature-rich and attuned to the quick, changing pace of the market.

Recently, several AMS providers have partnered with a select social platform vendor to provide a "recommended" social networking solution to their clients. In one instance, the social platform provider has not integrated with any system other than the one platform since the partnership was announced. The exclusivity of this agreement should definitely raise red flags to the consumer. An exclusive integration means the AMS provider is trying to clasp golden handcuffs on their clients so they can never leave. The frustrating thing around such a ploy is when asked if they integrate with any other AMS, the answer was evasive, "Yes, we've integrated with several AMS systems and can integrate with pretty much any." The words are very carefully chosen. Yes, they did integrate with other AMS systems (but there have not been any since the partnership was announced), and yes, they can integrate with "pretty much any" AMS platform—but it does not mean they will. The best question to ask is, "Since forming your partnership, how many other AMS platforms have you integrated with?" This should get the information you need, but beware of evasive answers.

The final advice with AMS-recommended integrations is to be wary of any platform that offers only a single solution and ensure the platform is portable, that it can move away from the AMS with you.

5. Pricing

There are three basic pricing models, each of which has its own pitfalls, so try to examine what is right for you. Here are some helpful hints:

a) **Per User:** What constitutes a user? You may have 10,000 members and 50,000 nonmembers in your database but only 1 percent of them may be active. If this is the case, are you paying for the inactive users? Also, what defines active? If you subscribe them to a listserver, does that make them active? If so, you might start off with 5,000 people subscribed and end up with a hefty price tag. Be very careful about the wording of such a model to ensure you are not setting yourself up for a sudden fare hike after the vendor knows your members are happy with the product. Personally, I do not recommend this model, as it makes me think you are being penalized for being successful.

b) **Per Community:** What is a community? This is typically any user or system-generated group. A core feature of the social web is the ability to break down your core membership into sub-groups, such as components, committees, or user-generated groups like a book club. Be sure you are not paying per group. It can become very costly, very quickly.

c) **Size of Organization:** This is my preferred model because it is fairly clear. Most nonprofits have published numbers, so charging by the size of your organization is usually pretty straightforward. Just be sure you clarify how the size of your organization is measured, and make sure it works for you. For example, you might have only 50 members but be a $10 million organization. Is the size of the organization calculated on the number of members or the annual revenue? Make sure you understand the model before moving forward.

d) **A La Carte:** This usually works in combination with per-user or size-of-organization pricing models. The benefit of this model is that you pay for only what you want versus paying for everything but using only a small portion. For example, if you want a social media-enabled listserver but do not want the file sharing to go with it, then why pay for it? Of course, the vendor that does not offer this option may argue that it gives you everything for a low cost, and it is not worth their time switching off certain features. It is easy to look at this from different perspectives.

6. Content Management System Considerations

Social platforms would typically be in a subdomain of your main website (such as community.rims.org is a subdomain of rims.org). This is a key consideration. What happens when you want to put the latest blog postings or discussion contributions on your main website? The best solution for this is webservices. Webservices allow you to easily grab content from your social platform to display on other websites. If you are using Microsoft Office SharePoint Server (MOSS) for example, then you would want .Net User Controls (web parts), which talk to webservices. The vendor of your platform should provide the webservices for the most common requests that can be consumed by your user controls (web parts).

User controls should also have parameter options that give you a little more flexibility with how you might wish to use the controls. Below is an example of just a single user control for "Latest Blogs" with all the parameters you might wish to use with it. Parameters are extremely important because they control not only the look and feel but also the security and other key attributes.

Parameter(s)	Values/Description
Display Photo	Whether to display the photo of the blog author(s)
Display Link to Profile	Whether to link to author's profile
User ID(s)	You can use this to show the latest blogs from a specific person or group of people. For example: the association president or perhaps everyone from your conference department.
Search Term(s)	You might want only blogs that contain the word "conference." (Perhaps this "blog roll" is intended for the conference website home page.). This can also be particularly useful with legislative blogs.
Member Type(s)	Should the latest blogs contain only blogs from people with member types, such as member, associate, or staff?
Community, Group, Networks	If your platform supports multiple communities/groups/networks, you might want to show the latest blogs for just that specific group. For example, if I created a member-generated community for "How to measure return on engagement," then, on the community home page, I might want to show just blogs that have been generated through this community.

7. SaaS Versus Installed Software

There is a common misconception that if you buy software, you need to install and run it locally, and so you will need additional bandwidth, server power, software licenses, and more. Many companies are now offering software in something called "The Cloud." If your provider offers Software as a Service (SaaS), this is an indication their product sits in the cloud. There are huge benefits and significant cost savings to cloud computing. The number-one thing to realize is that you do not have to buy the software. You simply pay as you go, typically on a monthly subscription basis.

It is not uncommon to find resistance from within your own IT department to this new model of computing; after all, it potentially means fewer servers and software they will need to support, maintain, and upgrade. One could argue that moving core functions to a SaaS model is comparable to progressive outsourcing. Many of those who have tried it, however, have come to recognize significant cost savings and a more manageable budget. SaaS provides huge value and allows your IT team to focus on what is really important to support the mission, rather than trying to apply patches and fixes, which they would not have to do if they were using SaaS products.

The number-one objection to a SaaS platform is the lack of integration and interoperability between your existing AMS and this new platform. For the most part, this issue has been overcome with the use of webservices. Many IT departments still do not realize how important webservices are and how they can provide integration with most other systems while having very little impact on performance.

8. International Considerations: Multilingual? Multicurrency? How Global Is It?

Many associations talk about world domination in their respective industries, but how realistic are your goals? When considering your social platform selection, it is important to consider your internationalization strategy. As discussed in chapter 13, most people assume the web and international simply equals multilanguage websites and don't pay attention to considerations such as currency conversion and date formatting.

When asking vendors about language considerations, be sure to see examples of your destination languages or at least have vendors show you a mock-up of how it would work. The right way to handle multilanguage websites is through resource files (where all of the context-sensitive prompts are stored in a file), so watch for this and ensure the prompts are not hard-coded into the system.

9. Event Management

For a techie, it is nice to imagine that everything can be done virtually. The reality, however, is that people generally do like to meet. Since the social web is all about groups of people with common interests, it is only natural they may want to meet in person from time to time. This was a key consideration for RIMS when selecting its social platform, as the goal was to enable chapters to create events in a common event calendar and allow for online registration and event management. Most chapters have monthly meetings, but they can involve all sorts of challenging registration options, including golf, round tables, and dinners. Each registration option might have different attributes; for example, a golf outing might allow the registration of a four-ball team versus a dinner, which might allow a single guest or the purchase of a full table. Things became more complex when a group of chapters got together to form a regional event that spanned multiple days with concurrent sessions.

For the organization, the event management needed to be simple enough for a volunteer to use but scalable enough to deliver enterprise performance and flexibility. Another key consideration was how payments should be handled. With the onset of PCI compliance, RIMS did not want to get into the business of processing payments on behalf of the chapters. Instead, the organization allowed chapters to set up their own PayPal accounts and follow a simple set of instructions that enables their websites to process payments through PayPal. The PCI and other credit card risks are then passed on to PayPal.

Event management may sound straightforward but actually can be a major issue, depending on your requirements. Do not be fooled into thinking you want only monthly meeting registration because invariably you will want more—if not for your chapter, then for something like the ad-hoc book club community that one of your members creates.

10. Basic Versus Advanced Functionality

The previous steps should give you an idea of the sort of things you can do with a solid social platform, but there is really only so much friending and group creation that can be done. It is always a good thing to ask the providers about the most creative things their customers have done with their software. This will give you an idea of how flexible their software is and how extendable it is. For example, the Social Networking and Media Association (SNAMA) recently launched a viral mentoring application that takes advantage of the friend/contact lists that members have built. Just as you can install an application in Facebook or LinkedIn, you can now take part in any type of application the association wishes to allow. In this example, a simple mentoring application was built; after selecting your interests/expertise, you are then sent to a referral tool where you are asked to invite five of your friends to take part in the application. After sending the referrals (which, in this case, were optional), the person was taken to the results page that displayed all the matches for prospective mentors/ mentees. The matches were charted/graphed and linked directly to the member directory search results, enabling members to connect.

This is a simple example of one of the most powerful yet under-used applications that a private social platform can offer. Enhanced networking and research are two key components to the social web. Of course, the platform is only as creative as those who are using the tools, but try asking your prospective vendor for real-time examples of how their customers have been creative with their applications. Few have solid examples yet.

Summary

The above 10 keys to success are only a guideline and are not intended to be comprehensive requirements. Every nonprofit and association is different, and the requirements should be aligned with what each organization wants to achieve from its platform. Social platform selection should not be taken lightly, as the restraints and constrictions of the platform can easily determine the ultimate success or failure of the venture. Consider using a professional who has extensive experience not just with the association and nonprofit world but also with the various platform offerings available. It is important to make the right decision and to have the internal buy-in to support and back that decision.

Useful tool: Sample Social Platform RFP: http://bit.ly/socialplatormrfp

CHAPTER 17

Go-to-Market Launch Plan

This chapter should help you determine your marketing and position readiness and provides an example of a Go-to-Market (GTM) plan. Before answering the questions, be sure to browse the plan to confirm that it will meet your basic goals and is in alignment with your mission.

Marketing/Position Readiness Assessment

Please take a few moments to answer some questions about your current or future marketing activities with regard to your new social networking community.

1. Have you thought about naming your community site?
2. Have you thought about the domain or URL you want to publish your community site under?
3. Is your community website a part of a greater organizational initiative to outreach or connect with your membership?
    a) If yes, have you named your initiative?
    b) If yes, have you visually branded your initiative (logo, banner)?
4. Have you thought about a specific design for your new community website?

5. Do you foresee having to move content from your main website into your community website?
   a) If yes, have you thought about how you plan to move relevant content that you have into the community website and tools?
6. If you are implementing microsite technology, to which components do you plan to offer it (e.g., chapters, sections, regions)?
   a) If this is your plan, have you created the designs to offer the various components?
   b) If this is your plan, have you assessed whether you need to migrate content from an existing site into a new tool? Have you already planned for this?
7. Have you informed your membership about this new community initiative/community website?
8. Have you performed a prelaunch survey of your members to help determine what their level of experience is with the social web or the web in general and their expectations of the new platform?
9. Have you prepared a postlaunch survey to test ease of use of the new platform; depth of use; how many of the new tools users are familiar with, have used, or know about; and whether expectations are being met?

Defining the Roles of the Constituents

Everyone within your community will have a role to play in its success. It is always a good idea to set expectations about who is expected to do what. For example, for a trade association, the board of directors might be asked to post an industry-specific blog once every two weeks as well as wear a ribbon at your annual conference that says, "I'm Connected." Make a list of stakeholders and start assigning them group and individual tasks. Here are a few examples of who your stakeholders may include:

- Board of Directors
- Volunteer Leadership
- Other Volunteers
- Marketing Staff
- Other Staff

Example Go-to-Market Plan

Approach

This go-to-market strategy has been formulated to promote the activities of the society, to encourage additional member participation, and to promote the work of the organization to prospective members with the intent of getting them to join. The approach of the GTM strategy is to leverage the available tools, ideas, and marketing plans to create a 12-month strategic approach that delivers the right messages to the various audiences with whom the society interacts and to empower the society to promote the work of the organization to enhance the member experience.

Goals

- Encourage user adoption of site.
- Promote member "professional branding."
- Present the society as a dynamic organization that has cutting-edge technology and has listened to membership.
- Appeal to various target audiences so people think, "There's something in this for me?"

Tools

Website

The new website will serve as the primary communication vehicle in rolling out promotions and items to the membership and other audiences that visit the site. With the flexibility of the homepage as well as additional online areas in which to promote the activities of the society and the work of the membership, the society will be able to promote activities such as upcoming events, solicit and encourage member participation, and collect and promote member spotlights. The use of imagery that resonates with various key audiences will serve as a main focal point on the website homepage so that on a monthly basis, website visitors (members, prospective members, students, general public) will have insight into what the society is promoting and the activities of the membership.

Videos

A key part of engaging membership is to constantly update material and find new ways to connect to them. Part of the initiative to communicate with them is to use multimedia formats. A brief series of video clips will be produced to:

- Introduce new society website
- Tour the site for members and nonmembers
- Demonstrate how to log in
- Showcase the most requested content

Ideas and Themes

Topics, concepts, themes, ideas to promote the society throughout the year:

- Upcoming annual conference
- Upcoming 50th anniversary of the society
- Quality campaign
- Awards—nomination entry deadlines
- Awards—designation announcements/Scholarship announcements
- Call for papers
- Publications/journal promotions
- Member-get-a-member campaign/Why did I join the society?
- Member spotlights—stories from the field, research/academic perspectives, enter the hall of members, lifetime member story, student member story
- Job announcements
- Promote for-the-public area
- "When I grow up..."
- Best find—series of personal stories of members, citing their "best find" on sites
- "Top reasons to practice..."
- "A day in the life"
- Recent research

Recommended Calendar/User Adoption Plan

The marketing calendar is a 12-month plan to promote activities and the work of the society. Additional activities can be built around each tool used in the GTM plan; however, the purpose of the calendar is to document and map the promotional concepts planned for the year. The society should use this calendar to promote upcoming activities within the organization and externally with the membership and other audiences who connect regularly with the society. Below are a few examples of what you might consider including. A more comprehensive list will likely require brainstorming sessions with the key stakeholders. Once you have a comprehensive list, ensure you attach deadlines as well as ownership.

Prelaunch Deliverables

a) Highlight:

- Campaign Theme: Uncover the New Society Website
- New look and feel that represents the organization
- New design allows for simple log in and makes it easy to locate information and navigate
- Greater opportunities for exposure—society mission/activities and work of the membership
- Open to all audiences interested in the industry of the society

b) Activities

- Complete beta testing.
- Send out blast notices that change is coming. Post article and small image on current website homepage to indicate that launch is coming soon.
- Announcement using communication vehicles (email blast? Newsletter?)
- Promote video briefs through homepage.
- Website homepage promotional area should have flash piece to cycle through new changes with link to learn more (links to article outlining new changes).
- Need images to promote "Uncovering the new website."
- Provide members with access to videos to help spread the word.

c) Material

- Webpage/article outlining new changes (Title: Uncover the New Website!)
- Press release to post and distribute

- Website debrief (Video)
- New website guide (PDF)
- New website guide (video)

Postlaunch: Go-Live Deliverables

- Press release article and webpage ready and posted online
- Videos made live (introduce new website; tour of site for members and nonmembers, login demo, most requested content)
- Spread word throughout membership. Ask task force committee to spread the word.

Activities for First Half of the Year

- Promote the work of the society and the new website; focus on new features; encourage members to look, submit information, share their pride.
- Promote the work of the society, upcoming conferences, plans for the remainder of the year.
- Promote annual conference, award applications/nominations, resources for students.
- Behind the scenes: The society should start collecting member spotlights/stories/pictures to promote in the latter half of the year. The society should sign up one member per month for this so that there are enough stories to collect and publish throughout the year and a repository upon which to build.

Activities for Second Half of the Year

- Membership—lead in to society milestone anniversary
- Postconference wrap up
- Member spotlights—scheduled for three months, so at minimum should have three members to spotlight
- Journals/publications promotion
- Membership with the society ("Why I joined the society"—stories/perspectives from current members, student members, retired members), promote the members hall of fame
- Promote activities over year; set up for next year and the milestone anniversary.

CHAPTER 18

Summary

Strategic Advantage for Nonprofits

Many for-profits are trying to encroach on the nonprofit space, and some are more successful than others. While nonprofits are typically slow to respond, they do have an inherent advantage over their for-profit competition—a built-in sense of community. The value of this should not be underestimated. For example, the publishing industry is going through a big change. Some subscription magazines are building niche social networks for their subscribers and promoting them as subscriber benefits. For-profit conference companies are taking a similar approach and attempting to turn an annual one-week trade show into a 365-day portal by providing niche social networks as attendee benefits.

The good news in this case is that subscribers and attendees typically do not possess emotional attachments as deep as those of dues-paying members or donors. This is one of the reasons associations and nonprofits have a much greater chance of being successful with the launch of a social platform than their for-profit peers. If launched in the right way, using a technology platform that is right for you, a social platform can enforce the sense of community that already exists and improve retention as well as attract new members.

Semantics

Depending on the culture of your membership, if you tell your members you have installed a social network, they may immediately think of bikini photos on Facebook—not exactly the sort of professional image you want to instill. On the other hand, if you tell your members how you've upgraded their member directory, there will be no misconceptions. Eventually they will learn how their much loved new member directory is actually a private social network and by that time, they will have used it, decreasing the chance of prejudging.

Brochure Websites to Member Websites

Unlike many websites today that focus on maintaining and updating a brochure type of content, primarily promoting what the association does and the benefits of joining, tomorrow's website is primarily focused on content created by members for members. User-generated content is key to the success of a member website. Great examples include the Corporate Compliance Association http://community.corporatecompliance.org and the New York Society of Association Executives www.nysaenet.org.

In both these examples, the home page is primarily composed of member-generated content supplemented by a small amount of association-created content. The home pages immediately display how active the respective communities are and provide a much more compelling reason to join. A member website should be seen as a recruiting tool. The value of the network is largely dictated by who is excluded from it versus those who are in it, thus promoting a more compelling reason to join. Of course, the key to any successful social initiative is the amount of engagement that is generated from it.

ABOUT THE AUTHOR

Andy Steggles is currently the Chief Operating Officer & Social Strategist for Higher Logic, LLC, a social media and mobile software company for associations and nonprofits. Prior to joining Higher Logic, Andy spent 10 years serving as the Chief Information Officer at the Risk & Insurance Management Society, Inc. (RIMS) where he headed among other things, their social strategy initiatives.

Prior to joining RIMS, Andy served in the Royal Navy from 1986–1996. In 1996 after serving around most of the world including the Arctic and Antarctic, Andy returned from a three-year tour in Hong Kong to London where he left the Navy and went back to school to study Computer Science at Brunel University. In 1999 after finishing his degree, Andy moved to New York City where he accepted a job as the head of technology for the Risk & Insurance Management Society, Inc. (RIMS). RIMS is an organization that recognized the value of innovation and allowed Andy to work on his own projects one day per week.

In 2003, after renting out his vacation home via the web, Andy realized the potential for vacation home referrals within the UK. In 2004, Holiday Home Rental, LLC (www.holidayhomerental.co.uk) was launched. Within a short time, the site grew from nothing to more than 20,000 rental properties and generated more than 150,000 pages of mostly user-generated content (UGC). Andy didn't know it at the time, but this UGC was his very early introduction to the social web. Shortly afterward, Andy's ex-military buddies (Royal Navy) started to contact him on Facebook and LinkedIn. This was his first proper introduction to social networking.

In late 2005, after launching more country-specific holiday home rental websites such as www.holidayhomerental.ie, it became clear to Andy how social media could directly affect the search engines. Fascinated with the potential business applications of the social web, Andy developed several software systems such as copytester.com which was designed to test the uniqueness of content to determine how well it would score in the search engines.

Social Responsibility

The author's proceeds of this book will be split and donated to the ASAE's Foundation to support association leadership as well as to various social responsibility projects as selected by Andy Steggles. To see more about these social responsibility efforts, see: http://bit.ly/socresp.

INDEX

T

U

V

W

Y